BE YOUR BEST COACH ...AND BEYOND

Steve Bavister and
Amanda Vickers

For UK orders: please contact Bookpoint Ltd, 130 Milton Park, Abingdon, Oxon OX14 4SB. Telephone: +44 (0) 1235 827720. Fax: +44 (0) 1235 400454. Lines are open 09.00–18.00, Monday to Saturday, with a 24-hour message answering service. You can also order through our website: www.madaboutbooks.com

British Library Cataloguing in Publication Data A catalogue record for this title is available from The British Library.

This edition, first published in UK 2003 by Hodder Headline Plc, 338 Euston Road, London NW1 3BH

Typeset by Servis Filmsetting Ltd, Manchester, England
Printed in Great Britain for Hodder & Stoughton Educational, a Division of Hodder Headline Plc, 338 Euston Road, London NW1 3BH by Cox & Wyman Ltd, Reading, Berkshire.

Impression number	10 9 8 7 6 5 4 3 2
Year	2007 2006 2005 2004 2003

Contents

U wouldn't worry what people thought of u if u knew how seldom they thought of u.

Series Introduction

Perhaps you have had an idea, or wanted to achieve something, but known that you not only need some skills but also help with taking the risk and doing it for real. Maybe you have thought 'it is easy for him/her but not for me . . .'

This series is written for people who haven't got the time (or money) to attend a long training course or who are not lucky enough to be managed and mentored by a star in the field in which they want to succeed. These books will be 'back pocket' resources that will inspire and give practical tips that you can read up on and use in the next few minutes. They will also help you feel confident in taking skills that you already have into new situations at work, home and the community.

Lesley Gosling
Q. Learning
www.qlearning.com

CHAPTER 1

What If You Were a Skilled Coach Right Now?

That is what learning is. You suddenly understand something you've understood all your life, but in a new way.

DORIS LESSING

Believe in yourself! Have faith in your abilities! Without a humble but reasonable confidence in your own powers you cannot be successful or happy.

NORMAN VINCENT PEALE

SEEDS WAITING TO GROW

All of us are natural coaches. And all of us make use of our natural coaching abilities – but to varying degrees. In some people, these abilities are already developed and mature. In others, the skills are more latent, less obvious, but waiting to grow – like a seed when it receives the right combination of water and sun. Even if you don't call yourself a coach, there will be many areas of your life where you may behave like one – and many occasions when you may have been a highly skilled and effective coach.

Progress now

List some of the ways people coach each other naturally.

No matter what your experience of natural coaching, it's likely you came up with a host of ways you and others support people. You may have thought about all of the times you have been a good friend to someone and given them hope. Hope leads us to possibilities, so that ideas and solutions become apparent.

MAKING CHANGES

When you are coaching, whether you label it that or not, you are likely to develop a special relationship with the other person. You may have specific meetings arranged for this purpose or you could use your coaching skills in all sorts of less formal situations. You will find yourself using coaching skills more often than you realize, such as giving your undivided attention to what someone has to say, being curious to find out how they think without making judgement, or asking questions that encourage them to explore their experience in a different way.

Progress now

In what ways are you a natural coach? Place a tick against each item that represents what you believe to be true about you. Then ask a friend or colleague to offer you their perspective.

- [x] I am a good listener.
- [x] I believe it is possible to learn something new every day.

- [x] I accept people as they are.
- [x] I believe mistakes provide an opportunity to learn.
- [x] I am really curious about life and people.
- [x] I get on well with people most of the time.
- [x] I am willing to challenge others where necessary.
- [x] I believe it is important to take time for others.
- [ ] I pick up on non-verbal signals that others often miss.
- [x] I am honest and straightforward with people.
- [x] I have a passion for people.
- [ ] I am comfortable with ambiguous situations.
- [x] I trust my intuition.
- [x] I am open to developing and changing as a person.
- [x] I value the contributions I can make.
- [x] I can be relied upon to follow through with my promises.
- [x] I have a creative and flexible approach to life.
- [x] I ask questions that get people thinking.
- [x] I am sensitive to the feelings of others.
- [x] I believe people have untapped potential waiting to be realized.

If you ticked fewer than seven items, you have some of the natural skills, beliefs and abilities that are represented in many good coaches. You also stand to gain a lot from this book. In it you will discover ways to develop your skills and new ways of thinking that will lead you on the path to becoming a great coach. If you complete all the exercises you will become clear about the sort of coach you want to become, strengthen your sense of what you believe about yourself as a coach and realize your potential.

If you scored between 7 and 14, your natural coaching skills are well developed. You are probably winning lots of friends by being available to support them when they need it most. Make a note of the areas you want to develop and start to explore the changes that need to be made. This book will help you to build on the solid base you have and take your coaching to a new level.

If you scored over 14 you almost certainly have a reputation for being a natural coach. You may already be working as a coach or thinking about it. You are likely to be open to learning new things about yourself and enjoy working with people. Every coach can always learn more. This book will challenge your thinking and round out your skills and knowledge.

CASE STUDY

DECIDING TO BECOME A COACH

Amanda remembers a time in the early days of her own development as a coach. She worked within a large organization and managed a large team who were based in remote locations across the UK. At the time she didn't always think of what she did as coaching. Yet when she reflects on it, that is certainly what she was doing. She spent hours on the telephone to various members of the team as there were limited opportunities to meet face to face.

One day, Karen, one of the team members, called. She wanted help deciding what job to go for to further her career. She had been agonizing over what to do for some weeks. Amanda listened for quite some time. Karen described three options she could take but felt torn between them. Amanda asked her questions that revealed what mattered most to her in her work and then suggested she take each option in turn and imagine for a few moments she were already in that role. What would she see around her? What would she be doing? How would it feel to do this role?

Within a matter of minutes she eliminated one of the possible roles. Although it had seemed like a good career move, she realized it would have made her unhappy and left her unfulfilled. Karen went on to explore the other two possibilities and made her choice. The relief in her voice was almost tangible. Amanda suggested that Karen reflect on it over the next few days.

Karen called a week later to thank Amanda and said she was clear about what to go for. Not too long afterwards she told Amanda she was applying for a new post. While Amanda was sad to see her leave the team, she knew that Karen was making the right move for her.

That experience was a turning point for Amanda. It had been so rewarding that she knew she wanted to spend much more of her time working with people in this way.

Progress now

One of the best ways to become clear about a goal is to picture it happening as vividly as possible, as if it were really taking place.

Picture a point some months or years from now. Trust your intuition, or gut instinct, to tell you the time in the future when you feel you have the coaching skills that you want. You may want more than just skills – you may want to become a successful manager getting the best out of a highly motivated team or a full-time coach with many clients on your list. Whatever you choose as your goal, you are a really effective coach.

What do you see in your mental picture? Who, if anyone, is around you? What do you hear? How does it feel to be established as a skilled coach? Take as much time as you want to fully explore your environment. You may find that it is easier to picture your surroundings than to get a sense of the sounds you might hear, or vice versa. Whatever you get will be useful to you, especially the feeling of having achieved what you set out to do. From this future place, think back to the time when you were reading this book. What message would you like to give that younger you? What do you know now that would have been useful to you then? Now think ahead. What does the future hold? What steps will you take to continuously improve your skills?

Spend as long as you like on this activity. Repeat it if necessary. The richer your experiences the more clarity you will gain on what you want from coaching and what sort of coach you want to be. Bear in mind that you can change and enhance your goals as you learn new things. The only limits to what you can achieve are the ones you place on yourself.

WHAT IS COACHING ANYWAY?

One of the problems with talking about coaching is the proliferation of definitions. A useful way of making sense of the situation is to think of the approaches as being on a continuum, with directive at one end and non-directive at the other.

In directive coaching, the individual is guided by the coach in how to do something, such as achieve a task or make a sale, whereas in non-directive coaching the learner takes greater responsibility for the direction of their own learning.

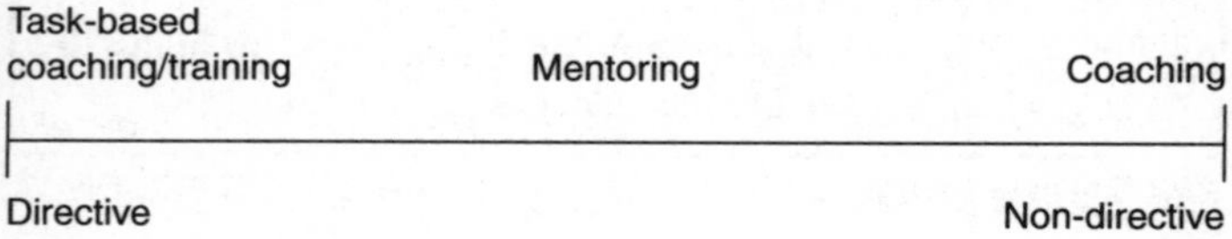

Task-based coaching/training — Mentoring — Coaching

Directive ———————————— Non-directive

DIRECTIVE COACHING

At the directive end of the continuum the coaching style is similar to training. The 'coach' – more aptly the trainer or teacher – directs the learning process, imparting knowledge and information to be absorbed. This can take place one-on-one or in groups. The person plays little part in determining what or how they learn. Having decided that an individual needs to be 'coached' in performing a specific task or skill, a manager may begin by giving an overview of the job and then break it down into chunks. Each step of the task is introduced in a logical order, with the manager often demonstrating how it is done. The individual then has a go at the task while being observed. The manager gives feedback that rewards what has been done well and suggests ways of doing things to create a better end result.

This type of intervention has an important place in business, but to call it coaching is to demean the great value of coaching at its best.

CASE STUDY

NON-DIRECTIVE COACHING

Tim Gallwey is well known for his work as an exceptional coach, both in the world of sport and business. In his book *The Inner Game of Work* he describes a point in his career when he became clear about learning and change and what makes them truly effective. 'My first insight into another way of coaching came the day I stopped trying to change the tennis student's swing,' he says. 'It occurred to me that there was a dialogue going on in the player's head, an internal conversation not unlike his external conversation with me.' What Tim had worked out was that the well-meant advice he gave was turning into part of the student's internal voice and rather than aiding them it was getting in the way of their natural ability.

This illustrates the clear difference between directive training and non-directive coaching. It also starts to reveal the power of not telling the person what to do. As the individual learns to trust themself rather than being distracted by 'shoulds' or trying too hard, performance naturally improves. One of the presuppositions of this kind of coaching is that the client has the necessary resources but may need help in identifying and using them with confidence. Another advantage of the non-directive approach is that the client owns their learning and is much more likely to follow it through because it is their own idea. The emphasis in this book will be placed on this definition of coaching.

DIFFERENT APPROACHES

There are a number of learning interventions – often labelled 'coaching' – that fall somewhere along the line between directive and non-directive.

Mentoring

Mentoring is often confused with coaching – and in business settings the two often go hand in hand. It is not unusual for new recruits and graduate trainees to be assigned a mentor, and some companies have formal mentoring schemes. Mentors typically use a mixture of directive – imparting advice or guidance – and non-directive coaching, allowing the person to discover answers for themself through the use of questions. The word 'mentoring' originates from Greek mythology, where it was said that Odysseus entrusted his home and the education of his son to his friend Mentor. Odysseus asked him to 'tell him all you know', hence the common understanding of mentoring as 'passing on experience and knowledge'.

Consulting

Management consultants generally take a directive approach. They go into an organization, analyse the situation and provide recommendations on what should be done. They bring with them specific knowledge and expertise – which is precisely what their clients want. Increasingly, however, consultants are also working as coaches, but they can sometimes find it hard to let go of 'being the expert', which is what coaching in its purist form demands, as the presumption is that the expertise lies within the client not the coach.

Counselling

The *Collins English Dictionary* defines counselling as 'a guidance offered by social workers, doctors etc, to help a person resolve social or personal problems'. A counsellor helps a client overcome blocks that have held them back in the past and may be causing problems in the present. Counselling mainly operates at the non-directive end of the continuum, with the counsellor creating a space in which the person can open up and talk about their problems. Counselling and coaching have a lot in common, but the key difference is that counselling primarily deals with problems whereas coaching is about enhancing performance.

Therapy

Therapy is concerned with the treatment of deep social or psychological problems or disorders, and embraces both directive and non-directive approaches. Some are orientated towards 'fixing' the past and others are solution focused – concerned with sorting out current problems. The work of most therapists is based upon a specific theory such as Freudian Psychodynamics, and this will shape their approach. Coaching differs from therapy in that the issues dealt with by therapists are generally more complex and deep-rooted. Some coaches are skilled in the use of Neuro Linguistic Programming (NLP) or Transactional Analysis, and use this training as a basis for enhancing their skills as a coach.

In the world of business, people are generally referred to an external counsellor or therapist where issues arise that are beyond their level of expertise. As you grow your skills as a coach it is important that you are able to differentiate between these things and are able to steer your clients in the direction that best suits their needs.

COACHING VS COACHING SKILLS

The main difference between coaching at the non-directive end of the continuum and mentoring or even counselling, is that the coach is operating out of a model in which they do not have the answers. A coach works from the presupposition that their clients have within them the resources to achieve what they want. Coaching used in this sense is about increasing awareness of what is happening for the client and widening the range of choices available to them. It is also about the client's becoming increasingly responsible for their actions.

Many people use the skills of coaching to good effect, but there is a difference between this and the unique relationship that is formed between a coach and client. In the latter the client is free to be themself and to express themself in the knowledge that what they do and say will remain confidential. When a manager meets with a member of their team to discuss the person's performance, they may use coaching skills. A good manager will listen well, use open questions and seek to find ways that will be effective in bringing about performance improvement. The difference here is that the manager will always have a double agenda: getting the job done well and ensuring that the team member is motivated and happy with the suggested change in approach. A coach operating at the non-directive end of the continuum, however, assumes that the client themself holds the answers that will work for them. The coach and the client work in partnership as equals.

From doing to being

As they become more experienced, many coaches find their sense of what coaching is all about changing. In the early stages, they are focused mainly on 'doing' – acquiring and applying the skills, knowledge and techniques required to be an effective coach, such as listening and asking questions. But over time, most coaches develop their ability to become self aware, and they start to think of coaching as a way of 'being', instead of something they do.

THE INFINITE POTENTIAL DEFINITION OF COACHING

Coaching is a collaboration, a partnership which helps people rapidly achieve clarity of direction, increase the choices available to them and be able to live their dreams. The coach believes that clients have infinite potential and the capacity to achieve fulfilment.

The Infinite Potential definition of coaching has much in common with the way coaching is defined by the International Coach Federation. The federation describes coaching as '. . . an ongoing partnership that helps clients produce fulfilling results in their personal and professional lives. Through the process of coaching clients deepen their learning, improve their performance and enhance their quality of life.'

These definitions are geared towards coaching as a non-directive approach. The focus is also less about remedial action being taken on poor performance and more about moving successful people forward more rapidly and supporting them in their quest to enrich their personal and business performance. Coaching is about learning and development and is linked to an improvement in performance of some kind. There is a goal attached to it, and attaining that goal brings about a positive change for the individual. In practice this means that, as well as having potential, each person needs to have a clear sense of purpose and a desire to attain their goal. If they want to achieve something, and if it fits with who they are as a person, their 'well of potential' is likely to be not only possible but also unstoppable.

DESIGN YOUR ALLIANCE WITH LEARNING

During the first session you have with a client you will normally agree a way of working that suits both parties in the coaching relationship. This is often called 'designing the alliance' (of which more later). You need to think now about how you would like to use this book in order to get the most from it. The information is organized in a way that gives you the chance to interact with the material as well as reading some thought-provoking content about coaching. As you work your way through the chapters you will be introduced to a wide range of approaches to coaching and will start to reap the benefits and enhance the way you coach.

CASE STUDY

TRICIA MACDONALD

Tricia MacDonald, an experienced executive coach, says: 'I work from the belief that everyone has untapped potential; that we all have capabilities that can be developed further, and that as our careers progress, the skills that will enable us to be successful fluctuate and change. My role as a coach is to provide my clients with the tools that ensure they achieve their goals and have the flexibility they need to take change in their stride.'

Tricia describes her role in coaching as being about helping people to achieve goals and handle the transitions we all face from time to time more easily. She thinks that what it means to be a coach requires a belief in human potential and that people are already empowered to achieve.

Progress now

Twelve ways to get the best from this book:

1. **Know what you want.** What's important to you about coaching? List at least 10 things and rank them in order of importance. If you could have only three, which would they be? Once you know what you want, your finely tuned senses will notice when you encounter passages in the book of particular interest.
2. **Be curious.** There are many ways in which you can be curious. For a start, you can be curious about what's in the book, what you will learn about coaching, and in what ways your knowledge, capabilities and skills will be enhanced most. And you can also be curious about the kind of coach you might become as you grow more accomplished.
3. **Be open to new ways of thinking.** By the time they become adults many people are fixed in their ways of thinking. While you may not agree with everything we say in the book, don't reject ideas simply because they're unfamiliar or don't fit with your current 'map' of reality.
4. **Challenge what we say.** Don't take everything we say as 'gospel'. Not everything we say will be true for every reader. Think carefully about the issues. Weigh up the pros and cons. Then take on board what seems to be of value, and leave behind what doesn't fit.

5. **Make notes (or not).** Some people find making notes aids their understanding; for others it's a distraction. Go with what works for you. You might prefer to read the book twice, getting the big picture without notes to start with and then go back for detailed study of specific sections.
6. **Do the activities.** You can only learn so much by reading, which is why lots of activities to stimulate your memory and imagination have been included. Do as many as you can. The more you complete, the more you will learn about yourself, and the better you will become as a coach.
7. **Seek support.** When you involve someone else in your learning you create leverage for change. By telling a friend, colleague or another coach what you plan to do, you make yourself accountable, increasing the likelihood that you will follow through and achieve your goals.
8. **Apply your learning.** Until you put new ideas into practice, they're just that – ideas. The only way in which you are going to be able to make a difference, and become a truly excellent coach, is by applying your learning. As you try things, you'll find you discover what works for you and what doesn't.
9. **Reflect on your progress.** You may not be aware of how much your skills and knowledge are improving. Stop periodically and take stock of the progress you've made. You may find it useful to keep a journal as you read the book, recording your thoughts at various stages. Looking back periodically will give you a greater sense of the ground you have covered.

10. **Enjoy your journey.** People learn most when they're having fun, so make sure you enjoy the time you spend reading this book and learning about coaching. The more energy and enthusiasm you bring to the book, the more you'll get out of it.
11. **Spread the word.** Coaching allows people to connect with their deepest values and beliefs and to use them as a basis for their actions. As more and more people give and receive coaching, so the ripples of its benefits will spread out into the wider community and impact upon society as a whole.
12. **Make contact.** The authors invite you to share your thoughts and opinions with them, tell them your success stories, or simply ask them a question. They can be contacted at coaching@infinitepotential.co.uk.

CHAPTER 2

What Does a Really Good Coach Look Like?

You don't see something until you have the right metaphor to let you perceive it.

ROBERT SHAW

Knowledge is only rumour until it is in the muscle.

NEW GUINEA PROVERB

CHARACTERISTICS OF GREAT COACHES

When you recognize that someone is good at what they do, how do you go about untangling all the elements that make them effective so you can learn from them? One of the best ways to answer this question is to have a session with a good coach and experience it for yourself.

Progress now

Identify two, three or more people you know or perhaps work with, who you regard as either a skilful coach or as having excellent coaching skills.

What is it about them that makes them really effective?

Recall the times when you have coached skilfully. What in particular did you do?

INFINITE POTENTIAL

Tim Gallwey, coach and author of *The Inner Game of Work*, says that, 'If someone can do it anyone can do it'. Once you have worked out precisely how one person does something it is likely that you can do it too, although there are clearly limitations on some of us for any number of reasons, both physical and psychological. Poverty and the impact of socialization can affect us in many ways too. They shape our experience in life, affecting our sense of identity, our education and inner beliefs about what we can achieve (this topic is developed in Chapter 4).

The authors call their company Infinite Potential because they believe people are capable of a lot more than they often think they are. Their passion for coaching arises from the fact that they believe it to be one of the most powerful tools available for unlocking that potential.

SELF-BELIEF

Pete really wanted to become a great coach. He already had skills as a manager, trainer and, of course, had life experience as well. The only thing holding him back was his own belief in what might be possible. His mind was full of how good other people were at this game. He seemed to think he could never reach the pinnacle that other coaches had attained. He drank in every experience and mopped up every piece of information. He was prepared to work at being a great client as well as a great coach and yet his goal seemed to elude him. Nothing seemed to satisfy his thirst. At a workshop for new coaches, the group leader asked him, 'What would it be like if you were standing on that pedestal with the people you most admire?' Pete's demeanour changed completely. Somehow just by imagining what it would be like, something shifted inside him. He made the change from disbelief to 'I am good enough' – recognizing he has the ability to be like the best coaches.

UNCONDITIONAL POSITIVE REGARD

I realise there is something I do before I start a session. I let myself know that I am enough. Not perfect. Perfect wouldn't be enough. But that I am human, and that is enough. There is nothing this man can say or do or feel that I can't feel in myself. I can be with him. I am enough.

CARL ROGERS CITED IN RACHEL NAOMI REMEN 'THE SEARCH FOR HEALING', IN R. CARLSON AND B. SHIELD (EDS) *HEALERS ON HEALING* (TARCHER, 1989, p.93)

The environment we grew up in and all the experiences we have throughout our lives contribute to our current perception of what is possible. If we are treated by others as if we are incapable of achieving our dreams, if our parents were overprotective, or if we do our best only to be criticized for not doing it even better, then we are likely to feel our confidence sapping away like water draining away from a leaking barrel.

Coaching – whether as client or coach – can be one of the keys that unlocks the door to greater self-belief, that plugs the leak in the barrel.

LEARNING FROM EXCELLENCE IN OTHERS

One way to learn about coaching is to study excellence in others. People who create excellent interpersonal relationships often speak eloquently and leave others feeling motivated and good about themselves.

It is possible to work out how anyone does pretty much anything by paying close attention to the patterns in their behaviour. The way that a good coach says things may be different from how other people say them in terms of either the words they choose or their tone of voice – and they may use different non-verbal signals too. (Chapter 8 gives you more ideas about how to refine your ability to become aware of how people experience life in different ways.) What you are aiming to do is to get to know what they are experiencing internally and what has to be in place in the external world around them. If you don't know them personally, you could glean information from a book they have written or observe what they do from a distance. Then you can take on their beliefs and ways of being a coach. Adjust what they do and believe to fit with your sense of who you are and what is important to you and start practising.

Progress now

What are the characteristics of a great coach? If you have the chance, talk to people you know to be good coaches or even ask them to coach you. Ask them questions to find out how they experience coaching. Uncover the underlying beliefs that drive their behaviour. See if you can add to their understanding of what they do through the quality of your questions – it's great practice for coaching.

- What kind of environment do they work in? Ask questions like: 'What do you take into account when you schedule a session?'
- What sorts of behaviour might he or she adopt? Ask questions like: 'How do you know what to do?' or 'What would stop you from doing . . .?'
- How would they be likely to feel inside when they are coaching? Ask questions like: 'What do you need to feel in order to . . .?' or 'Are you aware of any emotions when you . . .?'

Find out what they think about when they are coaching. What knowledge and skills have they acquired about their profession?

What is important to them? What do they believe about coaching?

How do they describe their role as a coach?

What is the difference that makes the difference in their coaching?

What patterns can you identify in the way they behave or experience things?

What questions can you ask to uncover aspects of their unconscious competence?

What is the underlying purpose that drives them?

IAN MCDERMOTT

Ian McDermott is a leading neuro linguistic programming (NLP) coach and Director of Training for International Training Seminars (ITS), which offers a range of courses for those wishing to enhance their coaching skills. He is the author of ten books, including *The NLP Coach*.

My work as a coach is about valuing individuals, teams and organizations, presupposing they have the capacity within themselves to deliver more than they thought they could – to surprise themselves, to challenge themselves, to delight themselves.

For me, coaching is a vehicle of service, one which enables me to honour those who choose to work with me. My aim is to find out what really matters to them, to engage with their aspirations, and together find ways these can be achieved in a practical way.

Coaching enables people to check in with themselves on some kind of regular basis, allowing them to take stock and find out what their position is – without being questioned into a point of view. This all happens within a structure provided by the coach – an interested party who does not have a content agenda, but has agreed with them a way of working that will enable them to clarify their own role and their own direction.

Coaching allows people to identify whether they are putting what is most important to them first – within their job, their relationships, their life, and probably all these different areas. Often they get a sense of reclaiming their life, not because it was out of control before, or they didn't have a life, but because they have a new sense of engagement with their life, where they reclaim what really matters and are acting with purpose.

As a coach you need, of course, to have a basis of skill, expertise and experience, but the most important element is that you can trust: you can trust yourself, and you can trust your coming together will be of value. If you can trust, and you have the experience to call upon, then you will be able to get out of the way. When you can get out of the way, you don't need to be there in the same way. You create a space in which you can be non-judgemental, you don't require a result, you're not out to demonstrate your own expertise. It's a space in which you and the person you are working with can explore, be vulnerable, be magnificent. That, to me, is the essence. When that happens, wonderful things happen – without necessarily being dramatic. You may know about them at the time, or you may only have a sense of them. When I am coaching I experience a settled feeling. I am at ease in the process, and whatever comes up is OK.

For me there is a spiritual aspect to coaching. It's a coming together where we may have apparently different roles, as coach and coachee, but it is a union in a way, and the union is one where we meet in a place which the person doesn't go to very often, or may only go in a specific setting. It makes it possible to live the sublime in this moment. Not because it's euphoric, not because it's dazzling, but because nothing more needs to happen than what is happening – because what is happening is all that needs to be happening. So there's a kind of acceptance about that. And the acceptance is part of the crucial experience.

For me as a coach there is also a kind of letting go. I don't need it to be a certain way. I'm not trying to make this person have a particular view, or reach a conclusion, or take an action. I don't require them to be something I can approve of even more. There's great freedom in being free of any agenda. By being free of an agenda, I can be present. That often seems to be communicated to the other person, who is more present, and in their own experience. There is a stripping away of the usual camouflage. Not because I am stripping it away. Not even because they are stripping it away. It just melts away.

Coaching in organizations encourages people to take stock and to take responsibility. The value to a business of a coaching culture is that over time it becomes more reflective, more curious, more proactive and ultimately more dynamic. And as people change the way they come at things, this can also then impact on society at large – showing up, for instance, in how we think about families, and the ways in which an effective parent might choose to coach their children.

Coaching is as diverse as most human activities. There are many different ways of being a coach and of coaching. It can take place in many different settings, and short periods of time can be just as valuable as longer sessions. At its highest level, coaching is one of the most influential tools available for encouraging a different way of thinking – and can have a fundamental effect on the way individuals and organizations function.

INTERVIEW

PETER OLIVER

Peter Oliver is Training Consultancy Manager at HSBC Bank plc. He manages a team of internal training consultants and is responsible for trainer development. He also works with all levels of management as an in-company coach.

Coaching, for me, is about being a catalyst. It's about allowing people to discover they have within them the resources they need to do what they want to do. The coach acts as a vehicle, enabling the client to get from point A to point B, with them defining where point A and point B are. It's not about the coach knowing what's right, or the organization supporting the coaching. For me, success is a useful, sustained change in your client. Sometimes you can see a change in someone instantly; sometimes it happens over a period of time. The reward for me often comes not from the coaching sessions themselves but returning weeks or months later and feeling how the atmosphere in the office is different. Sensing that it is a better place to work. That's the big reward. I facilitated an event for one client and his team of 56, who were queuing up at the end to say thank you, because I 'got through to the boss'. In fact, I just enabled him to discover another part of himself. He had the inner resources he needed all along, he just didn't know he'd got them.

It was valuable for him as an individual, but coaching also adds value to HSBC. I wish I was able to quantify the value – to say it adds £1.2 million a year or whatever – but we are not quite that clever yet. However, we recognize that we are a people business. We operate in a saturated marketplace, so any difference we can make with our people has the potential to make a huge difference in terms of safeguarding the future of the organization. It makes a difference when people find confidence in themselves they didn't know they had, skill sets they weren't aware of, and inner resources to get on and do things they felt other people could do but they couldn't.

There is far more coaching taking place at HSBC now than has been the case historically. We are moving in the right direction, but there are still big issues. We have been running Coaching for Managers programmes for some time, but perhaps we missed the point a little with some of the earlier programmes in that we dealt more with 'how to coach' and less with the 'why' – and even less with 'who am I as a coach?' That is the biggest issue for us now – getting that message across. There are many 'coaching' models bandied around the organization – covering a continuum from instruction right through to counselling – the question is: 'Where are we pitching the coaching?'

We have made a lot of progress at the more directive end of the continuum. In certain parts of the organization, such as regulated sales, we have field sales managers and field quality managers who are operating at the directive end of the continuum. The other extreme, the softer, more people-oriented approach, is less well developed – but improving all the time. The number of very senior executive level managers now having coaching, either internally or externally, continues to grow. The more they see the benefits the more that will impact on the culture, and encourage and allow the benefits of coaching to increase even further.

In an ideal world, every organization would have a 100% coaching culture. It should be second nature to everybody – whether they are the guy who mops the floor before the branch opens in the morning or the manager who signs off multi-million loans at the divisional management centre. It should be totally ingrained. I'm not sure we operate in an ideal world, and a coaching culture is something we can all strive for – but perhaps we need to be cleverer in the way that we make it happen.

Right now we are working on the coaching skills of the training team – not just on how to coach but how to deal with blockages

– with some of the things that get in the way. That is an area we hadn't covered well enough in the past. Most of our managers know about GROW or EDOF [an internally developed model: Explain, Demonstrate, Observe, Feedback] – but they're not really coaching. Anybody can use such models and work to a script, but coaching isn't about a script. What we do now is focus on where the blockages might be and what may be holding them back. We concentrate on what is important to the coachee.

We had a Coaching and Mentoring programme developed externally, and it has to be said 'it's the bee's knees'. It's a programme that stretches all of the trainers going through it, irrespective of their start point in terms of coaching experience. It's been described as an emotional rollercoaster, as an event that changes lives. I had somebody go through an assessment centre last week who had attended the programme in January 2002, and at the end of a fairly intense exercise he jumped to his feet, turned to walk out of the room, and said, 'By the way, that event in January changed my life.' That is the impact the Coaching and Mentoring programme is having on individuals. That they are now queuing up wanting to deliver it is another very positive sign. We could only get ten people on the first programme, and the fact that we're now oversubscribed many times illustrates the impact it's had. One of the crucial messages is: 'You are enough' –

INTERVIEW

you have the inner resources necessary to be a coach – and the clients are also 'enough' – they have the resources too.

For managers as coaches, it's about modelling. One of the things we've learnt in trying to launch any major initiative is that there is often a perception of 'something else coming out from the centre that is going to be done to us'. The way to change managers in the soft skill area is to model the power of the process – the effectiveness of that process. We have started to do that with our leadership programme where we run a session, which is a focused 25–30 minute one-on-one, but in a group context, where they get to explore any issue. By having the facilitator modelling the coaching skills at quite a high level during that process, the whole of the management population gets to experience the power of it. It's then a matter of working with them on a more regular basis so the skills are transferred. It's about developing a set of behaviours that have the desired impact. But what drives those behaviours? How do I know what to do? It's driven by what I believe about my skills. It's driven even more than that by what I believe about the skills of the person I'm coaching. It's not something that's behavioural. If it was it would be like a recipe card. Take 50 grams of this and three fluid ounces of that, whisk it and microwave for 3 minutes. We can't do that with coaching. If we could then we, and many other organizations, would have sussed it by now. There's much more to it than that.

My advice for other organizations wanting to introduce coaching comes in two parts. First, believe your people are enough – that understanding is absolutely critical. Second, you might have to convince them of that fact. You have to show them, demonstrate to them, that they are enough. We've done that through our Coaching and Mentoring programme, and it has changed lives completely, both in the workplace and personally. If we can do that in just five days, imagine what a coaching culture could do for an organization over years. It would be unstoppable.

So often in large organizations you hear about delegation but in reality things are not delegated. People are given no autonomy. They are given no authority. They may be given some responsibility but that's not what delegation is about. It's about truly empowering people. It's about letting go. It's about trusting them to deliver. My aim is to leave a truly empowered or entrusted collection of people behind me. Empowerment is a word that has been badly abused, and I'm working on a leadership model at the moment in which I talk about entrust rather than empowerment. The reason I've chosen the term 'entrust' is that I think it is about *total* empowerment. It is about giving people all they need in order to achieve.

The one thing I would say to any workplace manager wanting to make coaching work is that it needs to be at the top of the pile and not the bottom. When in-trays are three trays deep it's all too easy to put things like coaching aside and become very paper-driven. Emails have many benefits, but they can also be a tremendous bane. They get in the way of what many managers want to be doing, which is getting out and making a difference with their people.

Some organizations seem to perceive coaching as the latest fad, but I think you will find the truly successful companies ten years from now will be the ones which have totally integrated coaching. They will be the ones that have seen it for its true power and not as a passing fad. However, if any organization is going to invest in a coaching framework they need to ensure that it isn't just pretending to be a coaching framework, and is really focused on the development needs of its people.

The biggest issue in training is transferring the learning to the workplace. When you are training a bricklayer you tend to do it building walls. But management training often takes place in some kind of isolated training environment. Coaching is probably the single most powerful vehicle for transferring learning into the workplace environment that I've ever come across.

PETE COHEN

Pete Cohen is a motivational expert who created the Lighten Up Slimming Programme and Habit Busting. He is also the Life Strategist for GMTV and a successful author.

Coaching is about coaching people to coach themselves. You give them an experience, and allow them to figure things out for themselves – as opposed to teaching, which is telling someone what to do.

It makes life easier when people become their own coach, otherwise they won't do anything without being told what to do. They ask the coach everything. Coaching helps people become more responsible.

One of the things that Sven-Goran Erickson, the manager of the England football team, appears to have done is to get his players to be more responsible for themselves. That is the role of the coach.

My experience of working with athletes is that many are set in their ways, and they only seek out a coach when they have a problem – rather than wanting to get better when things are already going well. We tend to get comfortable with the way we are. We find something that works and then stick with it. The expression 'If you always do what you've always done, you'll always get what you've always got', sums that up pretty well.

Human beings tend to do the minimum they can get away with. The brain tries to protect us. It doesn't want us to get hurt. So we set limits upon ourselves and think we are those limits. People have invested a lot of time and energy to be where they are, and there is often resistance to change. The body and mind are made up of around 10 billion cells, and we know less than 5% of how it all works. We are infinitely more capable than we think we are.

When I'm coaching an athlete I don't work with the physical or technical side. It's all to do with the psychology – but the opposite of what you might expect. It's about not letting your mind get in the way.

What's the purpose of the mind in sport? Not to use it. If you've practised enough everything works perfectly. One of the first sports was called Zen archery, and the whole point was not to do with hitting the target, but about your mind being clear. When it's empty, that's when you let go. For me, that's what it's about with every sport. What I do is talk about that space where nothing else is going on, where you're totally at one with what you're doing. That's where you have to get to.

Mostly what I do is tell stories – and put ideas within the stories about how people like them have been successful, how people like them have got over problems. There's a lot of metaphor. I also talk a lot about the Eastern philosophy of sport, such as Aikido and Tai Chi, and the way the mind and body work together.

In addition, I work on self-confidence, on self-belief. One exercise I do is to get people to think about experiences in their life where they've performed exceptionally well – and run it all together as a continuous movie. Then I ask them: 'What would you say about that person if you were to sum them up?' Then you get them to go into the movie and say that affirmation to themself – 'I'm a great sportsman', 'I have what it takes', 'I have the power', or whatever it is – over and over and over again.

Coaching is worth doing because everyone needs support. We're sociable creatures. Just to know there's someone who supports you unconditionally, is there for you no matter what, is a very powerful tool, and is often the difference that makes the difference. It's great to have someone you can talk to openly and honestly about what you're experiencing.

Men in particular tend to be pretty poor about talking about how they feel. But doing so gives you clarity, and allows you to see things from a different perspective. The coach should see his role as a soundboard for the person, an observer to feed back what [he] saw. I don't think it's good for a coach to be critical – people don't respond well to that. Everyone's human. We all make mistakes. That's how we learn.

It should never be about the coach being right. They don't know what's best for the person. They might think they do, but being right is only one perspective. People sometimes go into coaching for the wrong reasons – because they want to tell people what to do. The best coaches have no ego.

If the person's struggling, there might be some benefit in providing more structure, and giving them specific things to do, but if they've reached a high skills level already, there's no need for that.

One of the great challenges and frustrations of coaching is the realization that you can't change people. They've got to want to do it themselves.

What I aim to do is get people to enjoy themselves. It's not the result that's important. They enjoy the winning, and they enjoy the losing, because they enjoy the doing. Often you have no control over the winning. You could be competing against other people, or against the clock. The only person you have control over is yourself. Being your best comes from focusing on yourself. If everyone enjoyed what they were doing, and it was the doing that everyone enjoyed, then everyone would be more successful in all areas of life.

The most rewarding aspect of coaching for me has to be when the person enjoys what they do so much they get lost in it. A transcendental experience happens where time disappears. They feel alive, powerful and sometimes magical.

What's equally important is that the coach enjoys the process. You've got to 'go first'. You've got to be passionate. You've got to create the space to be in the zone. When you're enjoying what you're doing when you're working with someone, you're going to find it a whole lot easier to put them in the zone as well.

INTERVIEW

JAN ELFLINE

Jan Elfline is a Certified Professional and Personal Coach and an NLP Master Practitioner and Trainer. She was among 40 professional coaches worldwide to receive the designation of Master Coach from the International Coaching Federation in 1998. Jan is founder of the NLP Coaching Institute, a US training organization that helps professional coaches develop extraordinary skills by combining NLP with business and personal coaching. Jan has worked as a Consultant, Coach and Trainer in the United States, Canada, Europe and Asia.

When I reflect on my skills as a coach it reminds me of when I first started gardening. I read a bunch of books and really learnt a fair amount about the subject. After a couple of years it felt like I was pretty good, but after five or six years I felt like I really didn't know much about gardening at all! I keep coming back to that for myself as a coach. I feel, at this moment in time, a strong need to reinvent myself. I feel I need to learn more, to explore more, and to somehow make my coaching richer than it has ever been.

As a coach my ongoing task is to become more and more aware of the subtle places where I am not modelling the life I want others to aspire to. I want to seek out the places where I am not being as honest with myself as I could be or where I am taking an easy path. My skills as a coach have definitely got past the beginner stage – even so, I wouldn't say I've achieved mastery. I have a label Master Coach which has to do with how long I've coached, how many people I've worked with, how many hours I've put in. I think it's a label that I would not take on lightly in terms of where I am in my personal development or development as a coach. I aspire to mastery; but I'm definitely not there yet.

When I coach I think of myself as a feather that is being blown around. The breeze is the client. I respond to that breeze – and yet I also have a presence of my own. It's about being flexible. It's also about realizing that I am not a great coach for everybody. There are people I will be very good with – we're a match together. If I'm not the best coach for someone, that is alright. It doesn't say anything negative about them or me. There is something about being who I am as fully as I can – expressing that as fully as I can to my clients and realizing that if that isn't a fit for them, or if my style isn't what's going to move them forward, they need to be with someone else.

Openness and flexibility are important to me. When I am at my best I am not formulating a question in my head, and I'm not either behind or ahead of where my client is. I am right there listening. I'm listening to the words, I'm listening to the content, and part of me is listening underneath to what their concern or worry might be and really allowing words to come out – even questions that are not completely formed. I may say to a client, 'This isn't going to be very articulate, but this is the gist of the question', and then I'll kind of blurt out whatever it is. Then the client processes it or they don't. They might drop it or take it and run with it. There's a quality of being present and noticing at many levels that is really rich. There is a flow about it.

Being present when I am coaching is important so that my own judgements don't get in the way. I bring my own sense of integrity or right and wrong to any interaction. This is a paradox. I am both modelling that and letting go of it at the same time. For example, I may have a judgement about a legal issue a client is making a decision about. I may have a strong feeling as an individual that this would be right and that would be wrong. Now, when I'm coaching if I bring that heavy-handedness into the interaction, I am not serving my client – it becomes another 'should' or 'shouldn't'. The decision comes from outside. When I can let go of that and let the client come to what is right for them, I have been surprised at how right a choice was for them that I would not have believed was the right way to go.

The moments I find most rewarding when I'm coaching are the little throwaway comments. I realize this client wouldn't have introduced a particular topic before, and now, after a period of months, they are. For example, I caught a client acknowledging his performance with some of his staff. It seemed like a small comment, very natural and organic. But if I compare it with when we started our coaching relationship, there is a big change. He would not have acknowledged his part in creating a system that worked. He would more likely have said he was lucky or 'the success was due to the other people around him'. It is those little moments that end up feeling big to me. Clients often haven't even noticed they are in a radically different place, but I notice partly because I'm only talking to them once a week.

The most challenging moments for me as a coach are when I have experiences or breakthroughs of my own that are closely related to what a client is going through. Then it is hard for me to hold back my advice. I do share bits of my experience. Coaches will share bits of their experience with their clients. But this is also when I run the risk of running my own agenda. I am so convinced that what worked for me or for another client is the answer. I run the risk of pushing it and I've coached long enough that I may not push it in very overt ways, but the sneaky ways keep coming up. There I am trying (at some level) to convince someone of something, to take this attitude or take this path. That's when I stop serving my client.

Coaching truly facilitates growth. There are few places in our lives where we have the opportunity to examine our choices consciously and with someone who isn't trying to influence us. The choices we make through coaching become very clear to us and are made for ourselves rather than because of 'shoulds' from outside. It is rare to find relationships like that outside of coaching.

Coaching is incremental. We have a choice about our state of mind, and we are responsible for it. Coaching is about putting that idea front and centre and saying, 'I know theoretically that I have a choice, am I going to make that choice every moment of every day.' There's a rigour to that. It's a rigorous process and I feel it should also be fun and there can be a joy about it.

For me the most important thing about coaching is the respect shown for the individual being coached. The assumption is that the client is the one with real control in their life and they will make good choices given the opportunity to think and talk through them. Coaching, as I practise it, is an opportunity for my clients to reflect and actively create their lives in an ongoing way week after week. It's not a single breakthrough or a cathartic event, rather it is the steady progress of growth.

I have to keep learning. The client knows more than I do about what works for them, and they will make better choices than I would make for them, so I need to be in an attitude of not knowing. The challenge is to not feel that you have to figure it out, or that you even could figure it out, or that you would have a better answer than the person over there. You do have different perspectives, and as a coach you are cheating your client if you don't offer them a perspective they may be totally unaware of. In sports coaching the coach is on the sidelines and the client is in the game – the one making the shots. The outcome is really in their hands. It goes back to trust and respect. It's the ongoing challenge of not trying to fix anybody.

For me, the core of coaching is being aware that we are choosing in every moment and every choice is like a drop of water that has ripples that go out. There's something about choosing the life you want for yourself and something about us together choosing the life we want for the planet. This takes many forms. Some people use words like spiritual or God or angels. Other people don't use those words but it is still a matter of consciously crafting your impact – being aware that you have an impact. It is about believing strongly enough that we do make a difference. Individuals make a difference. It could be the way you greet the person at the grocery store and treat them like a human being. It's something about treating people as people and not objects.

Coaching to me is an inspiration. As a coach I am always aware of how much courage people show in their own lives and how they are willing to make a hard decision or look seriously at their own feelings. When clients are openly honest with themselves I find it inspiring.

Progress now

Having dipped into the worlds of these experienced and successful coaches, what do you think makes coaching inspirational?

What are the qualities of a great coach?

What common themes did you identify?

What were the differences?

SUMMARY

We believe that great coaching helps to change people's lives for the better. They move forward faster and get greater clarity over what they want from life and work. Many great coaches have an approach that is aligned to what is important to them. They aim to live their values. Some of the qualities that stand out in the best coaches are trustworthy and trusting, congruent, curious, self aware, observant, caring, creative, flexible, tolerant of ambiguity, respectful, comfortable with not knowing what the outcome might be, listening in every sense of the word, able to be truly present for the client, and enjoying the coaching experience.

CHAPTER 3

What Do You Really Want?

People are not lazy. They simply have impotent goals – that is, goals that do not inspire them.

ANTHONY ROBBINS

If one advances confidently in the direction of his dreams . . . he will meet with a success unexpected in common hours.

HENRY DAVID THOREAU

Progress now

Reflect for a moment about something you really wanted, that was really important to you, and which you were able to do or get easily and almost effortlessly. What was it that unlocked the motivation and commitment to take action that is missing from all the tasks you never get round to?

The difference that makes the difference is that some goals are more compelling than others. They have a quality about them which creates energy and momentum.

For many people the first step is being really clear about what they want to achieve. When you want something enough you can often speed up the process by imagining you have it already. The more complete you can make your internal representation of what you want the easier it is to achieve it.

Every moment of your life is infinitely creative and the universe is endlessly bountiful. Just put forth a clear enough request, and everything your heart desires must come to you.

SHAKTI GAWAIN

The more specific we are about what we want the more likely we are to get exactly that. The reverse is also true. If we don't focus attention on anything we tend to end up with very little if anything at all. There is a saying, 'Where attention goes, energy flows.' If you are committed to something you are much more likely to create it.

When we are clear about how being a coach fits with what is most important to us in life it can make our goals irresistible. Whatever makes coaching important for you, the evidence shows that it contributes to increased performance, fulfilled potential, satisfied staff and has a positive impact on business results – so you are looking at a recipe for success. The best managers will not want to be left behind as more and more of their colleagues use coaching skills to good effect. Many coaches find they also learn a huge amount about themselves in the process.

HOW TO GET CLEAR ABOUT WHAT YOU WANT

The mnemonic SPACES provides a framework you can use to identify any outcome you want. You can use this to clarify your own goals and in your coaching to make sure your clients are creating sound, realistic and achievable goals.

Specific

Positive

Achievement

Control

Effect

Step into the future

Specific

The first step is to identify specifically what you want to achieve or change. If you want to be a great coach, what sorts of skills will you want to develop? In what circumstances will you be coaching? What kind of coach do you want to be? Will you be an executive coach, a life coach or a 'coaching manager'? When and where will you be coaching? How will you know you have attained your goal? When do you want to have started coaching? How will you go about doing what you want to do? Will it be part of what you do or all-consuming? You perhaps imagine yourself coaching in a specific type of situation or one that you find challenging in some way and want to be able to deal with more effectively. Ask yourself precisely what success would be like.

Being specific means you need to be precise and aim for total clarity over your goals. Becoming clear about what you want can be a great way to start practising your coaching skills – the questions you ask are likely to be similar to those you ask your coaching clients.

Types of coaching

Sports coaching

When people think of coaching, they often conjure up a picture of a sports or fitness coach. This is the person who keeps you on your toes and shouts at you from the touchline. Their focus is frequently on motivation. There is often a teaching, technical element but the best sports coaches go beyond that using a more psychological approach. Good sports coaching takes the performer beyond the limitations of the coach's own knowledge. In sports coaching the coach really is on the sidelines and the person out there on the field is making things happen.

Life coaching

Life coaches act as a catalyst in people's lives, helping them to bring out their best, know where they are going, and how they will get there. Life coaches tend to deal with individuals rather than working in a business setting, although the lines between the personal and corporate worlds are often blurred. Life coaching means exploring the whole of your life not just one aspect of it. Many executive coaches work in this way too, as they recognize the importance of taking a holistic approach. A change made in one area of your life is bound to impact on another.

Executive coaching

The Institute for Employment Studies defines executive coaching as '. . . an interactive process that is designed to help individuals to develop rapidly. It is usually work related and focused on improving performance or behaviour. It is a goal orientated form of personally tailored learning for a busy executive. The essential features of executive coaching are that it is short-term, time limited, paid for, goal specific, action orientated, and a personally tailored approach to learning. It utilizes feedback and offers some objectivity.' Executive coaching sometimes comes in other guises, such as performance coaching.

Some people talk about coaching a team to achieve better performance. Others think of coaching someone in how to take on a new task or to improve performance. You may have come across the idea of coaching being given to successful leaders or managers who want to enhance their skills. Executive coaching is often associated with those on a 'fast track' to senior management. It is also used where people are making a transition of some sort within their career or making life changes generally.

Progress now

What excites you about coaching? Imagine what it is like to be the kind of coach you want to be. Tap into what really excites you about the idea of coaching. What does it feel like to coach? How might others hear you describe what it means to be a coach?

This exercise is similar to previous exercises we have suggested you do. Each time you repeat this process you are likely to find that your sense of what you specifically want gets clearer and richer. Your aim is to make it as sensory specific as possible using pictures, sounds and feelings.

Styles or models of coaching

Checklist/tick box

One style of coaching commonly used is a checklist or tick box approach to performance improvement. This is where the coach gives guidance on what the person needs to do to improve their performance. The coach holds the client accountable for achieving a series of agreed actions, acting somewhat like an external additional conscience. While this style can give added momentum for a period of time it is less likely to be sustainable once the coaching partnership is ended. For some people it can be experienced as restricting and even prescriptive, but for others it can be just what they need at that point in time.

Skill/will

The skill/will model guides managers in deciding on the best approach to take when coaching team members. Skill relates to the experience, training and understanding the individual has of what is required of him or her. Will is about their motivation, confidence or desire to do it. The model can be represented as a matrix.

Skill/will matrix

High will	Guide	Delegate	Aim of coaching
Low will	Direct	Excite	
	Low skill	**High skill**	

The skill/will matrix is an adaptation by Keilty, Goldsmith & Co. Inc. of original work by Hershey and Blanchard.

Coaching in any quadrant area can help people become clearer and understand their underlying motivations and the way they might limit themselves. Where you have high skill/high will, coaching can expand horizons and help people to find out what will stretch them even further.

GROW

This model offers a simple sequence to follow when you are coaching, making it easy for a novice coach to use. GROW stands for Goal, Reality, Options and What is to be done next.

- **Goal.** The questions you ask here establish the short-, medium- and long-term goals of the client.
- **Reality.** This step is about exploring the current situation. Sometimes this will give the client an opportunity to express their feelings about some of the obstacles they are facing. At the very least it allows them to become clear about any problems.
- **Options.** This is where the client looks at the approaches that could be taken to attain the goal or overcome a hurdle.
- **What is to be done next.** Here the coach and client agree when action will be taken, who will take it and the client's commitment to carrying it out is explored.

Although the model is presented as a sequence, coaching can start and end with any stage in the process. In fact, you may find you move in and out of the various stages many times. With any framework there can be a temptation to race through each stage too quickly. Unless each step is fully explored you may find that an obstacle appears when you thought you had reached the finishing post – purely because you skipped spending time exploring all aspects of the client's current reality. The model needs to be used with awareness and responsibility.

For someone new to coaching, a framework like GROW can be a great boost to their confidence. With a little practice it soon becomes second nature and it is a good reminder of some of the key areas to cover when you are coaching. When used well this approach clearly works. One downside is that you could be tempted to 'follow the thread' provided by the model rather than the client. When it is used in a mechanistic way, there is a risk of you following your agenda rather than the client's and the questions you ask may not be the richest for them.

A detailed explanation of the GROW model can be found in John Whitmore's book *Coaching for Performance*.

Co-active

Coaching is about working in partnership – an approach that is sometimes called co-active. This way of coaching requires the active and collaborative participation of both the coach and the client. Co-active coaching is based upon the belief that the client has the answers within and that coaching unlocks a person's potential to maximize their success in achieving their goals. It is about helping people to learn rather than about teaching. For more details on the co-active coaching model and the skills and techniques used by co-active coaches, see *Co-active Coaching* by Laura Whitworth et al.

Now you have more understanding about the types, styles and models of coaching that are around you can start to create a very specific statement or series of statements that encapsulate what you want. The more clarity you get the more real and attainable your goal will become. A larger goal can sometimes be usefully broken down into manageable chunks. If your larger goal is to become a top coach you may want to create some sub-goals. Instead of saying 'I need to set up my first coaching session', you could say 'I will contact Joe by the end of this month and arrange a first coaching session.' This goal is specific and easily measured.

Positive

As well as being specific your goals need to be positively stated. The language you use – even to yourself – can have a powerful effect. Think of what you want in terms of what you do want rather than what you don't want. 'I will start my first coaching session this week', sends a positive signal to your unconscious mind rather than 'I don't want my first coaching session to be delayed by more than a week', which is negative. Your brain doesn't process the negative. When you hear or read a sentence containing a negative, your attention will go to the thing you are asked not to do before you even realize it. In this case the delay.

When you use positive statements you are focusing your attention where you want your energy to go – towards achieving your goal. You may think this doesn't matter that much, but try this simple exercise to find out how powerful negative language can be.

Don't think of your next coaching session

You probably found you had to keep thinking of your coaching session, even if you haven't got one arranged at the moment, in order to 'not think of it'. Precisely the opposite of what you were trying to achieve. The mind is no good at processing negatives, which is why it's important to keep everything positive.

Achievement

When you refine your goals, you will find it useful to get a sense of what it will be like for you to have achieved them. Think of other experiences you've had that demonstrate you can make what you want happen and go on to maintain progress. Getting in touch with the experiences you have inside of a job well done gives you a sense of what is possible. You may find that some of the skills and attributes you have which contributed to your success will apply in achieving your new goal.

Now think of the sensory-based evidence that will tell you that you have achieved the goal you have in mind. What will you see, hear and feel when you have attained it? For example, a manager who wants to improve her presentation skills will know she has achieved her goal when she can *see* herself smiling and relaxed after a successful presentation, *hear* positive comments from people afterwards and *feel* confident, alert and responsive from start to finish.

Control

Sometimes we want something that requires action from others to help us make it happen. For example, you may have as an outcome, 'I want to attract people to want me as their coach.' Achieving this goal would depend on actions taken by other people – it is not within your control. A better goal might be: 'I will build rapport with at least ten people and talk to them about the benefits I have gained through coaching.' In this example, the locus of control is with you. The goal statement you have created puts you at cause rather than effect.

You can think of cause and effect as being a continuum. At one end, cause, you are in control and feel free to achieve what you want. At the other end, effect, you find yourself dependent on others and a victim of circumstances outside of your control. Once you become aware that you are at 'effect' in any situation you are in a position to decide whether or not to change things by taking action to move yourself to cause.

As a coach, when you are working with a client you can ask them similar questions in relation to their goals. Do they have adequate control over the resources needed to achieve their outcome? What will they be doing to get there? Is it within their power to attain it? Often we are not in full control of the resources necessary to obtain our desired objective. For example, a client may wish to gain promotion at work. This decision is clearly not theirs to make, so the question becomes: 'What can I do to improve my chance of getting a promotion?' In this example, the client may make themself invaluable to their boss or take action to ensure their boss recognizes what they are adding to the team in order to help achieve this objective.

Effect

'Effect' is as simple as asking yourself, 'If you could have this, would you take it?' If your answer is an unqualified yes, then your outcome is likely to have been well defined. If, on the other hand, your response is, 'Yes, but . . .', then you may need to explore the areas where you have doubts or even ask yourself whether it is the right goal for you. For example, you may want to gain experience as a coach by arranging coaching sessions with six people during the next three months. When you reflect on this you might wonder if you can afford the time as other projects you have could suffer. Your refined goal might then become: 'I want to gain experience in coaching two people in the next three months', or 'I want to gain coaching experience by integrating coaching sessions with the team's career or development review sessions over the next three months'.

Effect is all about asking yourself searching questions. Only you know what you really enjoy doing. Is coaching something you can get really passionate about? Ask yourself these questions:

- Would I want to coach others so much that I would pay someone else to do it?
- If I could have this, would I take it?
- Does this really fit with what is important to me in my work and my life in general?
- Is it worth the time and effort it will take to achieve it?
- If there is a cost involved, is it worth it?

If your answer is an unreserved yes then your goal is probably right for you. If you have doubts in any area then you may want to refine it. If you discover a negative consequence to achieving your goal, think about how you could turn this into a positive opportunity. If what you want to do will have a negative effect on someone else, what steps can you take to reduce it to an acceptable level or eradicate it completely? (Chapter 10 looks at the whole area of maintaining a balance in your life.)

Step into the future

When we 'step into the future' we are checking out what it will be like to have our goal. This can be your first step towards acting as if it were happening now. Once you start to act 'as if' it can be remarkable how quickly your goal becomes a reality. One way to do this is to imagine yourself in the future, perhaps a month or so after you have achieved your outcome. From this future place ask yourself 'What do I see around me?', 'What can I hear?', 'How do I feel inside?' and 'Does it if feel right and comfortable?'

When you have a really rich idea of the future, and if you still feel the outcome is right for you, imagine being in a future place where you have achieved your goal and think back to the time when you were first considering this goal. What steps did you take to get there? What obstacles did you overcome? Who helped you along the way? Then reflect on how that information could be useful to you at the moment. If you are not entirely happy with your goal you can always review and change it. Simply look again at your desired outcome in the present knowing that you can step into the future to try the revised outcome whenever you want to.

You can use this technique in all kinds of situations. Using your imagination to go to a point in time that is after you have come through a challenging situation, such as sitting an examination, can help you to overcome anxiety and enhance your chances of success. Stepping into the future moves us past obstacles that sometimes seem insurmountable because the act of going forward assumes we will find a way round them.

Progress now

Imagine that your life is represented by an imaginary line a few feet in length on the floor. One end of the line represents the past and the other the future. This is your time line. Step on to it at a point that intuitively feels to you like the present and face the future. Once you have stepped on to your time line, walk slowly towards the future and in your mind's eye imagine some of the events that may take place over the coming months. As you walk forward, be aware that you are seeking a time when you have already achieved your goal. Stop when it feels right to do so and trust your unconscious mind to know where the right place to stop is. Once you are in this future time, again in your mind's eye, take a look around you. What do you see? What do you hear yourself saying to others? What are they saying to you? How does it feel to have achieved it? What is next? If it feels good, walk back down to the present and soak up the feeling of success you bring back with you. If the experience doesn't match up to what you had hoped, you may want to review your outcome and refine it to take into account any new information this exercise revealed for you.

ANCHORS

You have within you all the abilities you need to achieve excellence. However, you may feel confident and capable in one event, and in other situations these feelings may falter, and you may not be aware of the cause. Your beliefs about your abilities sometimes get in the way of your achieving the success you seek. One of the things that can help with this is to utilize 'anchors'.

An anchor is a stimulus that instantly 'fires off' a specific physiological or emotional state. The stimulus may involve a sight, sound, feeling, taste or smell. Your state is created by your sensory experience. Anchors change our state or the way we feel or experience something. For example, you may hear a piece of music and relive the images and feelings associated with an occasion when you heard it. Equally, if you are writing a report you can find yourself doubting your ability because of times in the past when people have criticized your work. Anchors usually operate at an unconscious level and are automatic in nature. The sensory stimulus triggers an internal chain of associations.

Anchors that make you feel good can be utilized in stressful situations. Before delivering a presentation to a room full of people you don't know, you can recall a time when you felt calm and confident. That feeling will then be there with you as you start to speak. The anchor associated to the memory will trigger automatically. The more you repeat the process of reliving that good memory as vividly as possible, the more calm and confident you will feel.

Not only can you design anchors that you consider might be useful, but you can also replace those anchors you would prefer to do without. Sometimes just becoming aware of an association will reduce its impact on you. If you go on to identify the experiences you had which trigger it, you can reduce its power over you still further.

Progress now

Step into the future once more using your time line. This time as you look around you imagine that you have a set of control buttons like the ones for your TV. Adjust the colour setting. Make the colours more vivid. Play around with the control button until it looks exactly right. You may want to make the image clearer or brighter. You might prefer it to be in 3D or like a panoramic film. Once you have got your image, turn your attention to the sound control. Turn the volume up or down – maybe adjust the tone or add background music. As you try out each way of experiencing your future, make sure you leave the control buttons set in the optimum place for you. Now adjust the control knob that adjusts the way you feel inside. Turn it up to expand your sense of satisfaction. Let that feeling seep through your body. Notice where it started and feel it move to every part of you. When you have the controls adjusted in just the right way for you squeeze your thumb and forefinger together. This acts as an anchor or reminder to your body and means that the next time you squeeze your thumb and forefinger again you will experience again the sensations you just created. The more you repeat this exercise the stronger the anchor will become.

WHY COACH?

Many managers working in a business environment think they don't need coaching. Their many years of experience as an effective manager seem to lead some of them to ask, 'What is the point?' In some organizations this attitude becomes a common theme especially where people equate coaching with rectifying poor performance. Because it can feel like a bit of an unknown quantity there is often an underlying fear that coaching will expose weaknesses or that reports or assessments will be passed on to superiors.

Good coaching never works in this way, so where does this perception come from? In those organizations that have embraced the concept of coaching it is evident that the best way to overcome this misunderstanding is to let the coaching itself do the talking. Once people have experienced coaching, and have started to reap some of the benefits, this resistance often dissipates.

BENEFITS OF COACHING

Benefits to organizations

- One of the most striking benefits of coaching is that it brings about sustainable change. Coaching is a form of development that is tailored to meet individual needs. Because the individual takes ownership of their experience, and is held accountable by their coach, it is much more likely to bring about lasting change.
- Coaching is cost efficient and in the business environment can enhance bottom-line performance. The impact that executive coaching can have on profitability is highlighted by a study conducted by MetrixGlobal. Its findings, based on 43 participants, concluded that coaching produced a 529% return on investment, rising to 788% when financial benefits from retention were taken into account.
- As Ian McDermott puts it, 'The value to a business of a coaching culture is that over time it becomes more reflective, more curious, more proactive and ultimately more dynamic.'
- Many companies use the strapline 'people are our most important asset', and that may explain why there has been an increase in the number of companies implementing a coaching culture. They

aim to obtain maximum leverage of their biggest asset. Rapid development of people leads to enhanced business performance.

- Staff retention is more likely. People want to work for organizations that care about their individual development. Equally, coaching can make it clear to someone that they are in the wrong job for them or maybe even the wrong organization. Either way, the organization gets to hold on to good people – the people who are likely to be motivated to achieve the organization's vision for the future. It retains people who fit with and are aligned with its culture.
- Coaching is one of the factors that helps make training sustainable in the working environment. Many training programmes have been greatly enhanced by the addition of follow-up coaching. Once the underpinning theory is in place, basic skills developed and beliefs and values relating to the subject matter have been explored, coaching can go on to develop and reinforce an individual learning strategy.

A Hay Group survey of 170 human resources professionals from around the world revealed that 70% of respondents believed coaching is more effective than training courses.

Benefits to people being coached

- Rapid attainment of goals – the combination of clarity, focused attention and a coach to remind you how you are progressing results in getting what you want faster.
- Enriched personal and business performance – when you are really clear about what you want you can go on to get more from everything you turn your attention to.
- Support when going through change, leaving the individual clear and motivated about the way forward.
- People who receive coaching develop many skills, including accountability, greater self-awareness and enhanced confidence in decision-making ability.
- Coaching enhances leadership capabilities generally, as the process of being coached builds some of the skills required of an effective leader, such as creating a vision of the future, and understanding what motivates the leader and the followers.
- Coaching gives more clarity about available options and therefore more focused career direction.

AUTOGLASS

When leading car maintenance firm Autoglass implemented a massive restructuring, executive coaching was used to support the firm's 20 regional managers. Each received three or four face-to-face half-day sessions over a three-month period, with telephone contact between if they needed it. Coaching was chosen over other options because the managers differed in terms of experience and skills, and coaching would cater for their individual needs with a tailored programme. The initiative not only had a significant effect on the company's business results, but also contributed to improved customer satisfaction reports. Furthermore, although the managers had initially been sceptical about the value of coaching, by the end they were converts – so much so that a significant number said they would pay for further sessions themselves if the company decided not to continue funding them.

Benefits to you as a coach

- For some people, coaching is a way of expressing something that is most important to them in life, such as helping others to develop. The great news is that you get to develop yourself in the process.
- You may be a manager who wishes to build a stronger team, retain core staff and see your people develop, grow and get a thirst for continual self-motivated learning. Anyone who leads a team of any kind will find coaching skills invaluable when they want to encourage people to give of their best.
- You might be a consultant, coach or trainer who has decided to broaden your skills in some way.
- You might simply have a desire to earn money through coaching. To earn good money it will help if you achieve excellence in your profession.
- You may just want to develop your interpersonal skills and enhance the relationships you have with other people in your life.

Progress now

Rate yourself, on a scale of 1 to 5 (where 1 is creating a negative impact and 5 is excellent work), on the following skills that can be developed through coaching. Come back to this list in two to three months' time after you have had the opportunity to use your coaching skills.

- Rapport
- Listening
- Time management
- Focus of attention
- Flexibility
- Questioning
- Accountability

To reap the many benefits of being a coach you will need to spend some time reflecting on how you want to operate. This will depend on what matters to you about coaching and how it fits into your job and life as a whole.

Progress now

Independent self-employed coach

- What do you want from your coaching?
- What sorts of issues do you want to work with?
- What kinds of issues would you pass on to another coach?
- What types of organizations do you want to do work for?
- What is your sense of identity as a coach?

'Coaching manager'

- What do you want from your coaching?
- What sorts of issues do you want to work with?
- What kinds of issues would you pass on to someone else in the company?
- What steps will you take to clarify for your client your dual roles of manager and coach?

MAKING WHAT YOU WANT COMPELLING TO OTHERS

For something to come across as compelling to other people it makes a huge difference if you feel enthusiastic about and inspired by what coaching has done for you. Enthusiasm breeds enthusiasm. If you can tell a convincing tale of what coaching has done for you and others, it is likely you will arouse people's interest.

Progress now

Put yourself in the shoes of someone you know whom you would like to have as a client. What would make coaching compelling for them? What would be important to them? What could you say in two minutes to get that person hooked on hearing more about what coaching could do for them?

CHAPTER 4

How Committed Are You?

If you find a path with no obstacles, it probably doesn't lead anywhere.

HARRIET BEECHER STOWE

The greatest danger for most of us is not that our aim is too high and we miss it, but that it is too low and we reach it.

MICHELANGELO

THE IMPORTANCE OF COMMITMENT

When you're not fully committed to a goal you are potentially setting it up to fail. If there are steps you're not willing to take, your commitment is only partial and you probably won't see things through. But what does it really mean to be committed? Most people think of commitment solely in relation to others – and would never dream of letting them down – but seem to operate out of different criteria when it comes to themself. They seem to think of themselves as less important than other people and don't keep their promises to themselves.

Progress now

How can you increase your commitment and move from thinking about doing something to actually making it happen? One way is to learn more about what happens inside you when you are really committed to something and then relate that to a goal or outcome where you would like to feel a greater sense of commitment.

Start by bringing to mind something you do for yourself where you have total commitment. Notice how you feel in your body. You might experience tension or relaxation in a certain area. Your breathing could undergo a change. There may be a sensation of warmth or cold, or perhaps a tingling sensation.

Now pay attention to your mind's eye. What do you see when you think about your total commitment? Do you observe yourself fulfilling whatever commitment you've made? Perhaps the consequences of having done so? Or maybe something else completely. Where in your mental 'field' does that image lie? How near or far away is it? Does it have a specific location? Is it in colour or black and white? Still or moving? Three-dimensional or flat? Clear or fuzzy? With specific boundaries or wrapping around you? Notice as much as you are able.

Finally, are there any sounds? Are you saying anything to yourself? Or hearing something else? If so, what is the voice tone like? Does it have a particular location, inside or outside your head?

Doing this exercise will help you understand how your brain 'codes' the experience of commitment. It may surprise you that all this is going on without your being conscious of it.

Now switch your attention to a goal where you would like to feel more committed. Carry out the same process, and note any ways in which the two are different. The secret to increasing your commitment to your goal is to match the modalities of your desire with those of the activity where commitment is not an issue. Bring your goal to mind once again and, step by step, work through the differences, making changes – perhaps the location of a feeling in the body, or the vividness of the image in your mind's eye. Once you've completed the process, you'll find your commitment to the task almost magically increased. Sometimes doing the process is all that is required, but you can repeat if necessary until it's fully 'wired' into the system.

WHAT'S MOTIVATING YOU?

Commitment may not on its own be enough. You can be as committed as you like, but if you're not motivated as well nothing will happen. If you think of commitment as the decision, the determination to reach a particular destination, then motivation is the energy that fires the engine and moves the vehicle in the right direction.

People often talk about motivation – or their perceived lack of it – when they fail to achieve something they want to do. Lack of motivation is often put down to a lack of willpower. That may be a convenient explanation, but it's not helpful. If you don't have enough willpower, you're always going to fail – so why bother?

Businesses, too, want people who are motivated – capable of meeting high standards and achieving prescribed targets in a willing and proactive way. One of the criticisms most commonly levelled by managers against their staff is that they're not sufficiently motivated – they seem to want to put in only the minimum effort.

You may have come across this notice on an office wall intended to spur the staff on to greater efforts: 'The floggings will continue until morale improves'. While it's obviously a joke, the underlying message is clear: if you don't do what the company expects, you can expect trouble. Most managers realize this approach simply won't work. You can't force motivation on anyone, it's something that's internally generated. You can nurture it – create conditions in which it might thrive – but you can't make it grow.

Progress now

Make two lists of things you want to do, some of which you may do already. On the first list record things you feel motivated to do easily and effortlessly. On the second include things where you find it hard to get motivated. Compare the two lists. What do you notice?

PLEASURE AND PAIN

One theory of human behaviour suggests that we are motivated towards pleasure and away from pain. In its broadest sense, 'pain' represents not just physical discomfort, but stress and emotional trauma, such as criticism, sadness, ridicule and hurt. If your parents or teachers laughed at your attempts to draw or paint, you're unlikely to feel motivated to pick up a pencil or brush now you're older.

One of the reasons money is so highly regarded and sought after is that it enables people to either avoid what they don't want or buy what they do – and the more money you have, the more choice and freedom you have. However, the situation is complicated by the fact that people experience and interpret things in different ways, as Anthony Robbins explains in *Awaken the Giant Within*:

> It is not actual pain that drives us, but our fear that something will lead to pain. And it's not actual pleasure that drives us, but our belief that somehow taking a certain action will lead to pleasure. We're not driven by the reality, but by our perception of reality.

While most people are motivated towards pleasure and away from pain, the majority have a preference for one of them – and use it in a wide range of different situations. These patterns of behaviour alter as we move from one situation to another. In this way they can be considered context specific. We all behave differently in different situations. How we are with our boss at work won't normally be the same as how we are with the children at home.

When people operate from an 'away from' pattern, they tend to avoid what they don't want or don't like. They often see things in terms of what can go wrong and where problems might lie. Those with a 'towards' preference on the other hand, generally move in the direction of what they do want and like. They tend to focus on the positive consequences of a course of action.

Neither motivation trait is better than the other, and neither of itself more effective. Whereas 'towards' motivation tends to be a constant and reliable spur as long as there is a goal to aim for, 'away from' motivation comes in peaks and troughs, can weaken when there is no perceived threat, and may lead to people suffering high levels of stress before they act.

CREATING LEVERAGE

Another way of creating momentum for change is by increasing the leverage in the situation. A simple way of doing that is to tell other people that you plan to do something. Once you 'put it out there', you're more likely to follow through because there are consequences if you don't, perhaps to your reputation or your self-esteem. Be careful, though, whom you tell. Only confide in people whom you know will be supportive.

You can also create leverage by focusing on what's important to you about coaching, rather than on the coaching itself. Focusing on a higher level can put energy behind what you are doing, because you are connecting powerfully to coaching at a deeper level within yourself – that is, your values, beliefs and sense of self. Of course, you may want to gain recognition and advancement for yourself along the way, but that's not your primary motivation, which is more to do with developing, helping and growing others. The stronger your values, the more powerfully they can leverage your motivation.

INTERFERENCE MATTERS

Many people find that although they know where they're going, and the car's all fired up and running, they never actually reach their destination – because something gets in the way. They might run out of petrol. They might get stuck in traffic. The clutch might go. Or they might end up in an accident. What then?

> # Progress now
>
> Reflect on things you wanted to do in the past but never did, or things you currently want to do but which are not getting done. What's the reason?

According to performance expert Tim Gallwey, first in his influential book *The Inner Game of Tennis*, and more recently in *The Inner Game of Work*, the situation can be summed up in one simple equation:

$$p = P - i$$

where p is performance, P is potential, and i is interference.

It is, he says, our own inner obstacles – such as fear of failure, self-doubt and unexamined assumptions – that get in the way. Much of this interference takes the form of conversations taking place inside our head – 'You're not very good at coaching', we may say to ourselves, or 'This person is going to be difficult' – with the resulting negative feelings causing us to underperform or achieve only average results.

It is only by addressing the 'inner game' that's going on inside us that we can hope to minimize the interference, maximize our performance, and so achieve our goals. When we're 'in flow' we're able to do things quickly, accurately and with economy of effort. But when we're distracted and our attention is incomplete, we make mistakes, and miss things.

Progress now

Reflect on the kinds of things you say to yourself, particularly when stressed or under pressure. How do they interfere with your getting what you want?

SELF-TALK

Self-talk, be it positive or negative, distracts – and the more you try to ignore it the more it distracts.

For the coach, this model provides a framework and methodology for not only helping others to deal effectively with issues getting in the way of fulfilling their potential, but also helping themself with the same kinds of issues. Sharing it with clients can provide a useful stepping-stone towards a deeper understanding. Alternatively, it can be used to surface hidden beliefs by responding to statements such as 'I/We can't do that' with questions such as 'What stops you?' or 'What would happen if you did?' A skilled coach will then be able to assist in the discovery and discarding of outmoded assumptions that are getting in the way. Where a less direct approach is preferred, the individual can be guided to compare the 'present situation' with the 'desired situation', and consider what might be needed to effect the transition, and what might get in the way. Doing so will often highlight the areas in which the inner game is operating.

Progress now

Write down at least ten ways in which you could hinder the development of your coaching skills, and sabotage your potential to be the best.

With all aspects of the 'inner game', awareness is the key. Start paying attention to what the voices in your head are saying and you will be on the road to tackling your interference. Notice when you're procrastinating in respect of a goal, and check the underlying beliefs that seem to be holding you back. As you discover the inner workings of your mind, so your resistance to follow through can sometimes disappear as if by magic.

GIVING IT UP

Often when we fail to follow through on something we want to do it's because either we're getting some benefit from the present situation that we're reluctant to give up or there's some downside to making the change we haven't acknowledged. Once again, these systems operate unconsciously so their effects are often not apparent until you start exploring what's going on.

Progress now

Sometimes we want to make changes and no matter what we do they still seem to elude us. If you're finding it hard to move forward with developing your coaching skills, pause and consider what hidden benefits there might be in the current situation you would have to give up. Then list any reasons you might have for not progressing things. You might also like to think about the potential downsides in becoming a more skilled coach. What, if anything, can you do about them?

A common fear among managers is that stacking more commitments on top of an already impossible workload will lead to mistakes and may possibly affect their personal relationships if they end up working longer hours or taking the job home with them. That's certainly a possibility if no action is taken to compensate for the time spent coaching – and there are no easy answers. We discuss this issue in more depth in Chapter 10.

When trying anything new, and stepping outside your comfort zone, you always expose yourself to the risk of failure – and that in itself can be sufficient for some people to be put off even trying. Don't stick your head over the parapet – it's likely to get shot off. But if you don't put your head above the parapet you won't get seen. And no one will remember your face when it's time for handing out bonuses or considering promotions.

If you're to make progress it's a good idea to say to yourself, 'I can live without that'. Sometimes you won't be willing to give up something – and the good news is that you don't usually have to. Most of the time you can find another way of satisfying that need. You could, for example, explore how coaching might enhance your skills as a leader, or become an in-company coach instead.

CHAPTER 5

Better Than What?

What would you attempt to do if you knew you could not fail?

Dr Robert Schuller

To improve is to change; to be perfect is to change often.

Winston Churchill

WHAT IS 'BETTER'?

In the last chapter you recognized your increasing commitment to achieving your goals and developed ways of being able to maintain and increase your motivation so you become an even better coach. But what exactly does 'better' look, sound and feel like? And what is the 'good' you are comparing it with? Where are you now? What are you good at already? And where do you want to be?

Progress now

Start with this self-assessment exercise.

Where are you now?

Where are you with your coaching right now? What are you good at already? Draw a line down the middle of a sheet of paper and list your strengths, abilities and skills on the left-hand side. Be as specific as possible.

Where do you want to be?

Now list the strengths, abilities and skills you would like to develop on the right-hand-side.

Wherever you are on the learning curve you'll hopefully have found it encouraging to recognize how much you know already. All too often we focus on what we can't do, rather than acknowledge what we can. This sometimes makes us feel inadequate and unqualified to coach, even when we have plenty of experience.

Although we've yet to discuss in detail some of the concepts and techniques of coaching, you'll already have a fair idea of where you would like to improve your abilities. While it might seem demotivating to focus on what you don't know, the value of this exercise is that part of you will now keep your attention oriented for information that will provide the development you desire – not only when you read this book, but in other things you do as well.

GETTING FEEDBACK FROM OTHERS

How do you know what your strengths, abilities and skills are? What evidence did you use for your self-assessment in the previous section?

The problem is that we can never really know ourselves in the way others know us and, since coaching is by its nature interpersonal and interactive, a good way to find out where you are at present is to get feedback on your coaching.

If feedback is given in the right spirit it is one of the most precious gifts you can receive. When you allow yourself to hear what people have to say you can use it for improvement in the future. Feedback is the royal road to learning, allowing us to build our confidence and continually enhance what we do. In fact, you might call it 'feed forward', because for the information to be useful it will have a future orientation – focusing on how things could be better rather than raking over what didn't work.

Progress now

Modelling feedback 1

Think of someone you know who is really good at giving feedback. What is it about the person, the way they are and what they do that makes it valuable and easy to receive their comments? What are the three most important things they do?

Modelling feedback 2

Now think of someone you know who is really terrible at giving feedback. What is it about the person, the way they are and what they do that makes feedback unwelcome and difficult to receive? What three things would enable them to give better feedback?

When people think of giving feedback they often go straight to the areas for improvement and skip the good parts. If you want to encourage someone to succeed in life it's just as important to let them know specifically what they've done well. If you go to as much trouble over this as you do with the negatives it will not only be more balanced but you'll also be letting them know precisely what they did that worked.

Ten top tips to better feedback:

1. **It's specific** – not general or abstract, and features particular incidents and moments as examples of what the person did or said. You're aiming for something they understand well enough to be able to replicate it.
2. **It's objective** – not based solely upon your opinion but founded on firm evidence. When you think about this, reflect carefully on the opinion part – it may be just your point of view. Make sure it's not just your desire to be right or your ego talking.
3. **It's honest** – not 'sugar-coated'. Rather than 'beating around the bush' it's expressed freely and clearly.
4. **It's simple** – too much detail at any one time is overwhelming and undermining. Too little on the things someone has done well will mean they won't know how to repeat their success.
5. **It's sensitive** – before you open your mouth think about how your feedback will feel to the person receiving it.
6. **It's practical** – and relates to something the person can actually do something about. If the other person can't change it

or learn from it don't bother – it will just feel to them like criticism.

7. **It's positive** – much of what the person did may have been good, and that should be acknowledged not glossed over. Some people shy away from praise or don't need someone else to tell them they've done a good job – they just know inside. This can mean they forget that other people have a different way of knowing – that others gather it from an external source.
8. **It's supportive** – and comes from a spirit of wanting to make things better. The best feedback lets the recipient know the giver really cares about them developing and wants them to succeed.
9. **It's about the behaviour not the person** – a comment on the particular task or action. The language you use will define the difference between these two. Choose your words with care.
10. **It's accepting and non-judgemental** – acceptance is all about seeing the real and complete person in front of you, someone who is making choices about how to behave and act based on their experiences. Uncritical acceptance is one of the greatest gifts you can give any human being.

RECEIVING FEEDBACK

When receiving feedback you need to be as receptive as possible. The most important thing is to avoid getting defensive. If you think of feedback as criticism, you probably won't get any value out of the exercise at all. If someone else is clumsy in the way they give you feedback, accept that they're doing the best they can and may or may not be aware of their shortcomings in this area. What you want is a 'reality check' – some clear, specific information about where you are in your coaching. Your weaknesses as well as your strengths. Your potential for improvement. Regarding feedback as an opportunity to learn something of great value will greatly enhance the experience.

Feedback sandwich

One widely used model is the 'feedback sandwich'. The idea is that you start by saying something positive, then say something negative or critical, and end with something positive. The thinking is that sandwiching the critical part with praise will soften it, and make it easier to take. In practice, because the technique is so well known, the recipient often discounts the positive comments because they are waiting for the inevitable blow when the negative is delivered.

NO SUCH THING AS FAILURE

One of the reasons people are fearful of feedback is because they equate it with criticism – and criticism with failure. And failure is something to be avoided at all costs. But there's another, more liberating way of thinking about all this, which is that really there's no such thing as failure, only feedback.

Imagine if babies tried to stand up for the first time, fell over, and said to themselves, 'I don't think I'll bother trying to learn to walk – it's too hard and I might fail'. Yet many adults expect to be able to do things straight away, and as a result don't try new things because they're afraid they won't succeed. Babies, though, don't experience falling over as failure. For them it's simply feedback about what doesn't work when you want to stand up – and they try again and again, refining their movements each time until they get it right.

> The inventor Thomas Edison is reputed to have tried hundreds of different materials in his search for the right substance for the filament of a light bulb. When asked if he got dispirited with each failure, he said no, that he was delighted to have eliminated yet another possibility and so narrowed down his search. It wasn't failure, it was feedback.

BUILDING THE FOUNDATIONS

In the same way that we often underestimate the skills we have at our disposal it's also easy to forget experiences which can be valuable in our coaching – such as times when we're really good at listening or asking questions. But such resources can become available to us by visualizing.

Progress now

Allow your mind to drift back to a specific experience you've had which, while it may not have been coaching itself, helped to build the foundations of your ability to be an effective coach. Start by watching yourself in your mind's eye as if you were in a movie, then 'step' into your skin and see, hear and feel what you saw, heard and felt when it happened. Now imagine your next coaching session, with that resource available to you.

Because of the way the brain works, what you imagine travels down the same neural pathways as what you remember, so visualizing 'attaches' the resources you have retrieved to what you visualized in your future – making them available for your next session and beyond. The more you access positive memories and 'anchor' them to events in the future, the more powerful you will feel when the time comes. The wider the range of resource experiences you use, the richer the skills and capabilities will be that you carry forward.

Progress now

List at least ten things that you are good at already – not just in your work, but in the rest of your life as well. Now pick the three you think you are best at.

Reflect briefly on how each skill could be valuable to you in coaching. Don't be too literal, let your imagination fly. Whatever your interests, the skills you develop in them will have some kind of value in coaching.

EMOTIONAL STATES

Managing your emotional state when receiving feedback is important – as it is when giving it, and during coaching in general. We all have times when we feel good, and there are other times when everything seems to be working against us and nothing seems to go right.

The difference between them is our emotional state, which changes many times every day. Most of the time we don't even notice. But when you're working with a client you have an optimal state you want to be in, which may not be your normal state, and it's useful to have some kind of mechanism to achieve it.

The easiest way of changing your state is by becoming aware of the triggers that create them. If you're clear about the state you want to be in to coach then it will be easier to achieve it. All you have to do is recall a time when you were in that state, and you will normally return to it naturally. If you start the process a few minutes before the session begins you'll be fully prepared.

HOW DO YOU KNOW YOU CAN BE BETTER THAN . . .?

Our beliefs tend to be a conscious expression of our core values and play a large part in shaping our attitude to our goals. Values are the internal standards which we use to direct our lives. We are consciously aware of some of our values whereas others operate at an unconscious level. These are the drivers that influence whether or not we think we can achieve something.

Progress now

This exercise, devised by Robert Dilts, allows you to rate your degree of belief in your ability to achieve your goal of becoming a good coach in relation to each of the following statements using a scale of 1 to 5 where 1 is the lowest and 5 is highest degree of belief.

1. The goal is desirable and worth it.
2. It is possible to achieve the goal.
3. What has to be done to achieve the goal is appropriate, ecological and fits with my sense of who I am.
4. I have the capabilities necessary to achieve the goal.
5. I have the responsibility and deserve to achieve the goal.

Review your response to each statement and use the rating to determine in which areas you're experiencing some uncertainty. Now you've brought this to conscious awareness, reflect on what needs to happen to move you forward. What small step can you take to change your belief?

THE POWER OF CELEBRATION

Celebrating success is much talked about in the world of business, but is less often experienced as an integral part of working life. If you're a manager with a team to coach, you can't afford to skimp in this area. It's worth being aware of the need to tell people when they've done something well in addition to providing financial rewards. This equally applies to you as a coach – you'll perform more effectively if you value what you do. It can make an enormous difference to you and your team's performance. As Ken Blanchard and Shelley Bowles put it in their book *Gung Ho!*, 'Enthusiasm equals mission times cash and congratulations.'

The money comes first because people only feel good about life when their basic material needs are satisfied. Next comes the need to satisfy what Blanchard and Bowles call the 'spirit'. It's not just about finding things to congratulate people about – although that's important – it's about letting them know what they do is valued and that they're making a contribution to something bigger. If people can see how what they do makes a difference on a grander scale they will be a lot more motivated to achieve it.

YOU ARE MAGNIFICENT

For some of you this may feel like a step too far. It's one thing to celebrate your successes and acknowledge your strengths, but it's a bit of a stretch to start talking about magnificence. Coaching is all about pushing back the limits of what you dreamt was possible.

Our deepest fear is not that we are inadequate, our deepest fear is that we are powerful beyond measure. It is our light, not our darkness that most frightens us. We ask ourselves, 'Who am I to be brilliant, gorgeous, talented and fabulous?' Actually, who are you not to be? You are a child of God. Your playing small does not serve the world. There is nothing enlightened about shrinking so that other people won't feel insecure around you. We were born to manifest the glory of God that is within us. And as we let our light shine we unconsciously give other people permission to do the same. As we are liberated from our own fear, our presence automatically liberates others.

MARIANNE WILLIAMSON, *A RETURN TO LOVE*

Progress now

This exercise, adapted from the work of renowned coaches Ian McDermott and Jan Elfline, gives you the chance to find out how others see the magnificence in you.

Ask two or three people you have coached, either formally or in the way we all naturally coach, to write a list of the ways they think you're magnificent. As a coach, it's important to believe in your own infinite potential. This makes you a great role model for your clients.

CHAPTER 6

Strategies and Techniques for Getting There

The best way to predict the future is to invent it.

ALAN KAY

The secret of getting ahead is getting started. The secret of getting started is breaking your complex, overwhelming tasks into small, manageable tasks, and then starting on the first one.

MARK TWAIN

HOW YOU DO ANYTHING IS HOW YOU DO EVERYTHING

There is much similarity in the way that people go about developing their coaching skills and the approaches they use in other areas of their life. Some people, for instance, get a feel for the basics and then just dive in. Others prefer to research thoroughly any new activity before attempting it for the first time.

By the time we are adults we have a limited repertoire of preferred ways of doing things. Where the approach we choose is suited to the task in hand, we find we're good at doing it; where it's not appropriate, we tend to be less successful. For this reason people who are flexible, who have more choices available to them on how to tackle something, tend to have greater success: they can use the tool that's best adapted to the job in hand.

Progress now

How do you tend to tackle jobs? When are your approaches effective and when don't they work? Which one will get you to where you want to go in coaching?

STRATEGIC THINKING

What do we mean by 'strategy'? Tad James, of Advanced Neuro Dynamics, expresses it neatly when he says that 'all our external behaviours are controlled by internal processing strategies – a strategy is what goes on in your head when you want to do something'.

The internal sequence you go through can be thought of as the steps in a recipe. You need to add the correct amount of each ingredient at the right time, blend them correctly, and then choose the most suitable cooking method, temperature and duration. If you add an ingredient too soon or miss it out, you won't achieve your goal.

Most strategies are established in the unconscious mind at an early age as people learn how to make things happen. By the time they are adults, people become aware of their strategies only when they don't work, and they have to rethink the way they tackle something.

The automatic way in which strategies work can have its disadvantages. Because they operate automatically you have little or no control over them. And once you've established a way of tackling a particular task that seems to work, you're likely to continue doing the same thing without reflection. Becoming aware of your strategies is the first step towards starting to take control of important aspects of your thinking and behaviour – and it can also be a valuable way of helping your clients when they're not getting the results they want.

Getting stuck in strategies that 'work'

Most people learning a new skill or developing an existing one focus on doing it right – and will often experiment with different ways of doing things. They try something out, observe how well it works, notice where it can be improved, and then make adjustments the next time they do it.

Sometimes, however, they hit upon an approach that seems to be effective the first time they try. While this can be good in that it delivers results straight away, there's always a risk that it will prevent the person from looking for other modus operandi and they will settle into a rut of doing things the same way.

Once they have a strategy that seems to 'work', people have a tendency to keep using it until it doesn't. Having reached a certain level of competence, the strategy drops out of consciousness and operates automatically. Thinking is required only when there is a problem. Moreover, just because a particular strategy produces results doesn't mean there's not a better way.

BECOMING AWARE

Coaches need to be aware of the dangers of growing stale and to look actively for ways of improving their existing skills and perhaps adding new ones. It's all a matter of reviewing, on an ongoing basis, what is often taken for granted – of constantly challenging yourself, and seeking ways in which things can be improved.

Awareness is the first step in dealing with a recurrent pattern. Once you know it's operating, and you start to monitor the way it's sabotaging your ability to achieve what you want, you can try out alternative options. Sometimes you don't even have to attempt to do anything different. Having become aware of what's happening, change occurs spontaneously.

CASE STUDY

IF WHAT YOU'RE DOING ISN'T WORKING, DO SOMETHING DIFFERENT

James was having problems building positive relationships with people at work. Encouraged by his coach to start paying attention to what was going on during his interactions, he came to realize that because he liked to be challenged himself he tended to challenge others. His intention was positive – to help them refine their thinking – but many found him intimidating and aggressive. More aware of the dynamics of the situation, he began experimenting with 'softer' ways of engaging with his colleagues and the relationships began to improve almost overnight.

REALITY CHECK

One of the problems of coming up with a strategy to achieve a certain goal is that people are not always realistic. Because they so want things to work out they can be hopelessly optimistic, and have a blind spot for what could go wrong.

One way of countering that possibility is to employ a technique made famous by animator Walt Disney which he called 'imagineering'. He broke down the creative process into three distinct phases, which he called Dreamer, Realist and Critic. The purpose of the Dreamer is to come up with new ideas. The Realist has the responsibility of giving them a practical expression. And the Critic considers possible problems. While all three elements are essential, they are distinct ways of thinking and difficult, if not impossible, to do effectively at the same time. You need a balance between the three roles. Many people have a Dreamer, and lots of creative things they want to do, but lack a Realist that enables them to come up with workable solutions. Others have no difficulty in making things happen, but don't have sufficient creative ideas in the first place. The problem for some is an overactive Critic which comes into play too early in proceedings so that an idea never gets off the ground.

Walt Disney actually went as far as having three different rooms in which he adopted the different roles. Physically moving from one room to another helped keep the roles separate. After a while, simply stepping into the Dreamer room would be enough to start the creative juices flowing.

Those familiar with the 'Thinking Hats' and 'Action Shoes' models developed by Edward de Bono will notice parallels with the Disney strategy. The Disney strategy can be used whenever creativity is required, and is equally effective when you are on your own or in a team.

Progress now

1. Start by thinking of an issue where you would like to put a strategy in place to achieve a particular goal.
2. Designate three locations for the different phases. Taking three pieces of A4 paper, writing Dreamer on one, Realist on another, and Critic on the third, and placing them in different parts of the room is perfectly workable.
3. The first stage is to associate existing experiences with each of the phases with the locations you have marked out.

4. Before you enter the Dreamer area, spend a moment or two recalling a time when you were able to creatively come up with new ideas without inhibition. In your mind's eye create an image of where you were and who was with you. Notice what was being said, including the tonality and volume, and become aware of how you were feeling. Then, holding on to that experience, step into the Dreamer space, and enjoy the sensations for a few minutes.
5. Step into a 'neutral' area – i.e. one away from the three designated locations – and think about something else briefly.
6. Move over to the Realist area, but before you enter it recall a time when you were able to think realistically and constructively about an idea and develop an effective action plan. Again in your mind's eye create an image of all the circumstances present in that situation and become aware of how you were feeling. Then, holding on to that experience, step into the Realist space, and enjoy the sensations for a few minutes.
7. Step once again into your neutral area and think about something else briefly.
8. Move over to the Critic area, and before you enter it recall a time when you were able to be critical in a constructive way. Once again in your mind's eye create an image of the circumstances present in that situation, and become aware of how you were feeling. Then, holding on to that experience, step into the Critic space, and enjoy the sensations for a few minutes.

9. Step into your neutral area and think about something else briefly.
10. Bring to mind the issue you would like to work with.
11. Step into the Dreamer location and generate as many ideas as you can. Visualize yourself accomplishing the goal as if you were a character in a film. Feel completely free and uninhibited. You are not concerned whether ideas are possible or not. Do not analyse.
12. Now take all the ideas generated and step into the Realist area and begin to develop a plan. Some of the ideas will probably be dropped and others modified. Look for positive ways in which ideas can be brought together into a realistic series of actions.
13. Then go to the Critic position, and thoroughly evaluate the plan. Will it work? What might be able to go wrong? Is there anything missing?
14. Turn the criticism you have into questions for the Dreamer, and step back into the Dreamer location to come up with solutions and alternatives to address them. Again, let ideas flow.
15. Complete the cycle as many times as necessary to come up with a plan you are happy with.

FROM A TO Z OR A TO B?

It's easier to practice our Oscar acceptance speech than to get up and go to an acting class.

MARIANNE WILLIAMSON, *A RETURN TO LOVE*

Patience is a virtue – and it can be an extremely valuable one when it comes to getting what you want. Sometimes it's possible to have your dreams fulfilled without waiting, but more often than not it's a matter of reaching your goal as a result of the cumulative effect of many small steps. Scientific breakthroughs often follow many months or years of painstaking research – and it will almost certainly be the same for you in respect of your coaching. Little by little your listening skills will improve, your ability to ask the right question at the right time will be refined, and your command of the essential coaching concepts will be enhanced.

One way of maintaining your motivation through this period is to monitor the incremental progress you're making by reflecting after each coaching session how things have gone, and recording your thoughts in a journal. Looking back periodically will give you the opportunity to observe how much progress you've made, even if it's not immediately obvious to you.

WISHCRAFT

In her book *Wishcraft: How To Get What You Really Want*, Barbara Sher introduces a technique for creating a step-by-step plan of how to achieve a large goal by breaking it down into smaller sub-goals. Starting with your ultimate goal, work backwards to identify the things you need to do to achieve it. At each point ask yourself: 'What do I have to do first?', and then 'Can I do this today?' If the answer is no, then you identify what needs to be done first. By completing this process you will not only create a chain of events that leads to the achievement of your larger goal, but also have the first step which you can do immediately. You may find there are several strands of action you'll need to progress in parallel, and that some activities you plan to do are interdependent.

Clearly this technique is valuable when working with clients as well as on yourself.

USE YOUR INTUITION

The strategies discussed so far are logical and procedural. If you prefer to work more intuitively, try the following techniques which are not as structured but are just as useful and practical.

Images of the future

Take a large sheet of paper and draw a picture of where you are now and another of where you want to be, i.e. moving from good to better in your coaching. The drawing can be as abstract as you like, and monochrome or vivid according to your preference. All that matters is that it makes some kind of sense to you. Then add further elements to the drawing to represent the resources or stages needed to get from the present situation to the desired state.

Preparing your inner self for coaching

Sit somewhere comfortable where you will not be disturbed. Close your eyes and relax. Focus only on your breath as it goes in through your nose and out through your mouth. Notice how your breathing rate shifts and you become more and more relaxed.

Imagine you're in a cinema and the screen in front of you shows a beautiful and peaceful place. In your mind's eye step into the picture and experience this place. Hear the sounds around you and feel what it's like to be there. Enjoy the sensation of calm which surrounds and fills you and know that all the inner resources you need will be available to you whenever you need them. When you're ready, return your attention to your breathing and gradually return to the room.

This process will help you prepare mentally and emotionally for coaching. Use your creativity to adapt it in any way that works best for you.

STEAL THAT STRATEGY

The good news is that strategies, like computer programs, can be installed, updated, modified or deleted to meet changing needs. In an earlier chapter we discussed the way in which you can improve your coaching skills by learning from more experienced coaches, and nowhere is this more true than when it comes to strategies. When you have the opportunity to talk to the person rather than simply observing them, you can go beyond copying their external behaviour to replicate instead the mental processes underlying it. This is much more powerful.

What are the person's beliefs about what they are doing? How does it fit with their values and sense of self? What processes do they use to formulate their plans? With a cooperative coach and sufficient time, asking precise questions will allow you to elicit their strategy in full.

By replicating what they do, you will be able to produce the same result as they do – not immediately perhaps, but with practice and commitment you will steadily increase your mastery.

AFFIRMATIVE ACTION

Because the unconscious mind plays such a major role in strategy and motivation, it is a good idea to 'reprogram' it regularly – and one quick and simple way is through affirmation. All you have to do is repeat a phrase a number of times during the day to focus the attention of your unconscious mind on what it is you want. Over time it will become an integral part of who you are and what you do.

The more specific you can make your suggestions, the more likely they are to take root. As ever, frame them positively, and keep them achievable. Here are a few suggestions to get you started:

- I am a skilled coach.
- I am good at asking the right question at the right time.
- I am an attentive listener.
- I am making a difference when I coach others.
- I am good at putting people at ease.
- I am open to feedback.

CHAPTER 7

Better Knowledge

You cannot teach people anything. You can only help them to discover it within themselves.

GALILEO

Knowledge of the self is the mother of all knowledge. So it is incumbent on me to know myself, to know it completely, to know its minutiae, its characteristics, its subtleties, and its very atoms.

KAHLIL GIBRAN

WHEN TO COACH

One of the problems with coaching is that it's widely perceived as remedial – that people only need coaching when they're underperforming. In the corporate world, however, some 'high fliers' are either allocated a coach or choose to engage one themselves. There is an increasing recognition of the value that coaching can bring to high achievers in accelerating their career path and working with them on their business goals. A good coach will tell a senior executive things which those closest to them often don't dare to say – and this can be invaluable. Some coaches observe executives in action and base coaching sessions around the real issues their clients face.

In an ideal world everyone who wanted it would receive coaching on an ongoing basis. Having the opportunity to articulate your thoughts and expand your awareness of yourself in a safe and supportive relationship makes personal and professional development not only possible but also virtually inevitable.

USING COACHING WITH YOUR OWN TEAM

How does the kind of coaching described so far work when you're face-to-face with the reality of expecting a specific standard of performance and it doesn't materialize? It's extremely difficult, if not impossible, to be a coach in the true sense of the word with people who report to you because of 'position power'. The fact that you are the boss, with the power to set the person's performance rating, determine their pay level and, ultimately, invoke disciplinary procedures and have them sacked if you are not happy with their performance gets in the way. Everyone wants to look good to their manager. But coaching depends to a large degree upon the coachee's willingness to discuss areas of their work and aspects of themselves with which they would like to move forward. Opening up about that kind of thing to their supervisor can feel, to some people, tantamount to admitting they can't do their job.

For managers to be effective in developing their team using coaching, they need to be able to separate out in their own mind and actions the different roles and responsibilities they have within the company – and have their team recognize them and accept them as separate. Because that's such a difficult thing, a number of key coaching tools and concepts can't be used or won't be effective – which limits what can be achieved. For that reason we refer in this book to managers using coaching skills with those who report to them as coaching managers – to make a clear distinction between coaches who operate without the limitations of position power. There are many benefits in using coaching skills with your team even if it's not a full coaching relationship. Managers can, of course, be coaches in the full sense of the word outside their area of responsibility, such as in another department or for a peer.

A manager's different roles

- Manager – charged with the smooth running of your department or the business as a whole, as well as meeting business targets
- Performance manager – responsible for setting objectives and developing the skills and abilities of your staff
- Motivator – getting the best from people, creating an environment that helps keep them committed to the job

- Delegator – cultivating excellence in delegation will encourage your staff to grow and make it possible for you to take the next step up the corporate ladder
- Mentor – if you 'worked your way up' you'll be able to share your expertise and experience to help those seeking to develop their own abilities
- Leader – executives are expected to be not just managers but also leaders, capable of developing and articulating a vision for their area of responsibility
- Diplomat – not an official role, but one that usually goes with the territory, skilled in dealing with political infighting
- Team player – able to work harmoniously and effectively with other individuals and departments
- Coach – coaching is increasingly recognized as an essential management skill

While coaching can clash with some of the roles listed, it complements and enhances most of them. In a manager–subordinate relationship there can be a conflict of interest. Some managers quite literally let their team members know when they are changing hats by telling them that they are now coaching. But this is often met with scepticism. The key to managing this balancing act is for the manager to act with integrity and to behave in a way that matches their inner beliefs about the individual needing to feel safe enough to be completely open. As a coach it is important to recognize whether or not you can create this feeling of safety. If you can't, you may not be the best coach for that person.

All coaches as well as managers need to be aware of when they are coaching and when they are mentoring, as the two are often regarded as the same thing, especially by those with a directive view of what coaching involves. In practice a manager wearing a coaching hat will behave differently from one wearing a mentoring hat. One of the best approaches is to allow the person to decide by marking out the distinction with your language. 'It sounds like you want me to respond from a mentoring perspective . . .' or, 'Would you like me to coach you on that?' The confidentiality of information divulged by the coachee must be remembered at all times.

Everyone is a unique individual, and managers will differ in the degree to which they are able – and, in part, willing – to separate out these roles. This will influence enormously their potential effectiveness when it comes to coaching their team.

In some organizations the conflict between managers' roles is overcome by using peer coaching rather than leaving line managers to take on the whole responsibility for coaching their own team. Peer coaching involves two managers, often at the same level of seniority, agreeing to offer coaching to each other's team members. It tends to work best where there is the greatest geographical distance between the coach and the coachee (it can be carried out by telephone), and for this reason smaller companies may choose to use external coaches.

CARROT AND STICK APPROACH

People seek to avoid pain and move towards pleasure, and it's true that many grew up being punished when they did something wrong and praised when they did something right. But such a 'command and control' approach fails to take account of people's increasing need to feel more in charge of their own destiny, to be fulfilled, and enjoy what they do.

People need to feel motivated to perform – you can only make them do it up to a point. A 'carrot' in the form of a pay increase or promotion will of course be an inducement, but is unlikely to be enough to encourage them to operate at their peak potential on an ongoing basis.

That's where coaching comes in. By working one-to-one with your team you can help them build awareness so they can maximize their motivation – not so that you can exploit them, but so that they can move towards what's important to them. Because they're drawn to it, they'll naturally be motivated to do it. In addition, it will not only make life easier for you but also pay dividends for the company.

COACHING MYTHS

Coaching takes up a lot of time

In fact, the opposite is true. There is an initial investment of time – which is how the myth originates – but once the benefits of coaching kick in, people are more self-reliant and self-directing, and they take up less of the manager's time.

Coaching is just another way of teaching

Coaching could not be more different from teaching. Coaching enables a person to find out the best way of doing something for themself whereas teaching involves someone outside telling them how to do it.

Coaching is only for people who are struggling

The fact that the chief executives of many leading companies have coaches is enough to nail this myth – but it persists. Coaching can help everyone improve their performance.

Coaching is about giving advice

While this is certainly true of traditional sports coaching, modern business and life coaching is quite the opposite. Instead of giving advice, the coach asks questions, supporting the client in using their own resources to come up with a solution that is right for them.

The results from coaching take too long to achieve

People vary, and so do the issues with which they are working. For many clients a series of six to twelve one-hour sessions over a period of three to six months produces tangible results.

People prefer to be told what to do

Once people have tasted the benefits that coaching can give them, most prefer to play a part in determining their own destiny.

Coaching only benefits the person being coached

Certainly the person being coached does benefit, but so does the company, because the employee is better motivated, is more likely to fulfil their potential, and will want to keep working for a company that cares about them. What is often not acknowledged is the degree to which the coach also benefits from the coaching process in terms of personal and professional growth.

Coaching undermines the expertise of the manager

The tradition in the UK, and in some other countries, is that of the manager as expert, and one of the challenges lies in managers' being willing to let go of that and to allow everyone to contribute.

COACHING AT A DISTANCE AND FACE TO FACE

Coaching is carried out in two main ways: face-to-face and over the telephone. Email or internet coaching are other options, but much less common, since they are much slower and do not operate in real time. Within companies, where the coach and coachee work together in the same building, and often the same office, face-to-face is the norm. Where geography mitigates against this, the telephone is often used. Even though external coaches are geographically distant from the clients, they offer both face-to-face and telephone coaching.

Some world-class external coaches work mainly by telephone, since it makes best use of their time and their clients can be from anywhere in the world. That's also true of some clients, whose globe-trotting lifestyle fits better around making a call from a mobile to their coach when it's mutually convenient, rather than having to be in a specific place at a particular time.

However, the majority of business and life coaching is carried out face to face, and even when subsequent sessions will be over the telephone, the two parties usually meet for the first appointment. Doing so helps establish rapport and builds trust.

DURATION AND FREQUENCY OF SESSIONS

Many businesses contract external coaches for two-hour or half-day sessions, because that is the most productive and cost effective arrangement. When the coach is working with a number of people in the same organization they may be booked for the whole day, and conduct two or three coaching sessions one after the other.

Telephone coaching sessions typically last 45 minutes to 1 hour. Most coaches find that the longer sessions enable their clients to discuss issues in greater depth, and more progress is made. Some coaches, however, prefer a shorter time frame because they feel it helps focus the attention of the coachee, and again more progress seems to be made.

Coaching sessions often have a natural 'arc', after which the client feels that the issue being discussed has been completed. It's impossible to know in advance how long that will take. If the client feels that something has been achieved before the session is scheduled to end, it is often better to draw things to a close early rather than to leave a new issue hanging.

Frequency is also a matter for agreement between the parties. Generally, appointments are every fortnight, which is sufficiently often to maintain momentum, but not so frequent that they become a pressure to the coachee. With anything longer than two weeks between sessions the coaching can struggle to achieve very much.

Progress now

If you're a manager who coaches, think of ways in which you can best use your time in respect of coaching.

Whatever your situation, you may want to think about 'ring-fencing' the coaching sessions, so they actually happen on time, each week. If you allow them to get moved – or, even worse, cancelled – it sends a clear signal to the coachee, and everyone else around, about how much value you really place on coaching. People judge you by your actions, not your words. For coaching to work it requires dedication and commitment – on both sides.

GETTING OFF TO A GOOD START

Coaching relationships sometimes founder because they've not been set up well. Problems and misunderstandings can surface later if important aspects of the coaching have not been made explicit and there are differing views of what should be happening.

Ethical conduct

One of the most important things to make explicit at the start is the rights and responsibilities of both parties. Most external coaches give clients an agreement to sign which details the terms and conditions under which they work, and this often forms part of the contract. It sets out some of the ground rules and parameters of the relationship. It is not definitive, and deliberately not so, because the coaching sessions themselves are 'co-created' by the client and the coach working together. Companies with a formal coaching system usually have a similar document.

One of the key issues is that the coach acts ethically. Most independent coaches are affiliated to a professional organization such as the International Coach Federation (ICF). As a condition of their membership, they subscribe to a code of conduct or code of ethics, the terms of which are spelt out in some detail.

Examples of the ICF Standards of Ethical Conduct

- I will conduct myself in a manner that reflects well on coaching as a profession and I will refrain from doing anything that harms the public's understanding or acceptance of coaching as a profession.
- I will identify my level of coaching competence to the best of my ability and I will not overstate my qualifications, expertise or experience as a coach.
- I will, at the beginning of each coaching relationship, ensure that my coaching client understands the terms of the coaching agreement between us.
- I will not claim or imply outcomes that I cannot guarantee.
- I will respect the confidentiality of my client's information, except as otherwise authorized by my client, or as required by law.
- I will obtain permission from each of my clients before releasing their names as clients or references.

- I will be alert to noticing when my client is no longer benefiting from our coaching relationship and thus would be better served by another coach or by another resource and, at that time, I will encourage my client to make that change.
- I will avoid conflicts between my interests and the interests of my clients.
- I will not give my clients or any prospective clients information or advice I know to be confidential, misleading or beyond my competence.

The full list can be found on the International Coach Federation website at www.coachfederation.org/ethics.htm

One of the central ethical themes in coaching is putting the client first and protecting their interests. It's only when coachees know that everything they say will be treated as confidential that they will share their innermost thoughts and experiences. Confidentiality and trust are essential for a coaching relationship to work. If there's no bond of trust, coaching can be no more than superficial.

CASE STUDY

INTERNAL COACHING AND CONFIDENTIALITY

Confidentiality may be complicated by other factors, says Peter Oliver of HSBC Bank plc

'One issue that becomes more difficult when you are coaching internally is confidentiality. It's not just guided by conscience, but also by rules, regulations, and job requirements. In a large, bureaucratic organization we have instruction manuals for just about everything – and to some extent they dictate what you can and can't keep in confidence. If something is revealed that constitutes a breach of those regulations, an internal coach would have to make a judgement whether to disclose or put their own career on the line by maintaining confidentiality. That makes coaching more difficult, and sometimes more complex.

It's easy for us to say that managers should create a coaching scenario that is confidential by saying, 'Forget temporarily that I'm your reporting manager'. It doesn't quite work that way, and even if it was completely 'ring-fenced', I don't think the coachee would believe it in the majority of cases. Within HSBC it works best when the coach is not the line manager – where they coach someone from another part of the business, or come from training and go into a branch or department.'

The issue of confidentiality is more problematical for internal than for external coaches – the latter will usually make it clear that they will not keep confidential anything a client discloses that is illegal in nature. However, a potential conflict of interest for external coaches arises from the question, who is the client? Is it the company which pays the invoice, or is it the person being coached? Experienced independent coaches will discuss this issue with the company up-front and make their position clear – which is usually that they cannot divulge anything said to them by the client in confidence.

One way of operating that satisfies both the coachee's need for confidentiality and the company's need to be kept informed involves briefing the person who contracted the coaching of general themes and trends, as agreed with the coachee. This only works, however, when you're coaching a number of managers from the same team otherwise confidentiality is still broken.

When you're coaching in-house, it's all too easy to break your commitment to confidentiality by accident. Trust is hard won and easily lost. Betray one confidence, and no one in the company will trust you again, or be willing to be coached by you.

Respect

Respect is another extremely important issue in coaching. People know intuitively when they are respected and when they are not, and react accordingly. If you're to be a successful coach, you need to respect all the people you work with all of the time in every way. Their opinions may not be the same as yours, but they deserve to be respected, even if you disagree. The same is true of their values and beliefs. You will support them more effectively if you also respect their limits. The rate at which they may be willing to grow and change is for them to decide, not you, and you need to respect that.

When you coach your own staff, as long as you do it willingly and with their interests at heart, it is a tangible demonstration of the fact that you respect them and value them. By taking time out of your busy schedule to listen to them, work with them and support them, you are building a relationship in which everyone benefits.

THE FIRST COACHING SESSION

There are many ways of starting a coaching relationship, but most involve getting together for an initial, exploratory session. Getting to know the other person first, and finding out what's important to them, is time extremely well spent. Some coaches call their first meeting with a client an 'intake' session, others a 'discovery' or 'contracting' session. It generally has more of an agenda and structure than the coaching sessions that are to follow, and is often longer – two hours is not unusual, and sometimes half a day is allocated.

In the initial session you will want to talk about the way in which you are going to be working together. Some people will mistakenly expect to be passive recipients of your 'wisdom', and may be surprised to discover instead that you conceive of it as a collaborative process. The authors of *Co-active Coaching* call this kind of coaching relationship the Designed Alliance, and describe it thus: 'The relationship is "designed" because it is customised to meet the exclusive needs of the client. It is an "alliance" because both players are intimately involved in making it work.'

Far from being a piece of clay that's moulded into the shape the coach thinks is right, the client is the one who defines the shape they want, based on the dreams and aspirations they have for themself, using the coach to help them achieve their goal. Because the agenda is set by the client, the coach will use questions such as, 'How would you like to use me as your coach?' to find out more about what the client has in mind. One of the implications of working this way is that responsibility for the coaching is shared, and the client plays a more active role in shaping the process. This means their commitment and enthusiasm are more likely to be engaged, increasing the potential for a positive outcome.

The Designed Alliance should never be regarded as something finished or fixed, but rather as something fluid. As the coaching relationship progresses, the coach encourages the client to redesign the alliance as necessary to adapt to changing circumstances. Few people will be used to consciously shaping their relationships in this way, and may find it strange to start with. But having grown used to it they are likely to find it empowers them in designing their relationships with others too in ways that are more fulfilling.

Checklist for an intake session

- What will happen in this session
- Check client's expectations of coaching
- Discuss how you coach
- Confidentiality issues
- Ground rules
- Designing the alliance
- Anticipating setbacks
- Establishing the primary focus for coaching
- Gaining an understanding of the client's values
- Exploring the bigger picture – how their issue relates to the rest of their life
- Scheduling appointments
- Feedback
- Accountability
- Are we right to work together?

Exploring the client's world

The intake session also marks the beginning of an exploration of the client's inner world that will last the whole of the coaching relationship. The coach needs to help the client bring to consciousness things of which they are normally unaware. Getting someone to think aloud will allow them, in Tim Gallwey's phrase, to 'eavesdrop on their own thought process' – and may help them advance towards their desired outcome. Simply ask open questions: What's important to you? How do you see your work, your company, yourself? What motivates you? Where do your interests lie? What are your dreams?

What is important is that you are genuinely curious about your client and what they are telling you. You are not there to judge or to assess them. Your role is to focus on supporting the person to come to an understanding of what they want, and on encouraging them to work out how they want to get there. It's not the responsibility of the coach to offer advice. Rather, the coach will ask questions that assist the client to come up with a solution themself. However, you will almost certainly want to give them feedback about what you notice and experience – and in doing so provide them with honest, neutral information that can aid their decision-making process.

If you are coaching a colleague, you may already know quite a lot about them. This can be a problem as you start with preconceptions, which you should as far as possible set aside.

Some coaches give clients forms to fill in and bring to the first session or have available for discussion in the case of telephone coaching. Those trained or qualified in tools like MBTI, Birkman or 16PF will often use questionnaires to find out more about the person. One of the fastest and easiest ways of beginning this process of exploration in a relatively structured way is to use the Wheel of Life Inventory and Values Elicitation Process.

The Wheel of Life Inventory

There are eight sections in the wheel, each labelled with an aspect of the person's life, for example Health, Money, Romance. The idea is to produce a visual representation of the balance or imbalance in a person's life. The centre of the wheel is 0. The outer edge is 10. Ask the coachee to draw a line across each sector to indicate their current satisfaction with that particular aspect of their life. So if they're

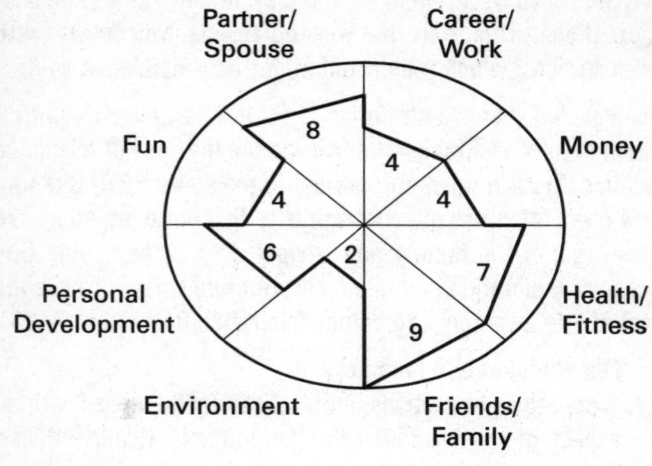

Wheel of Life

blissfully in love they might give Romance a 9. It can be helpful if they also write in their scores for each sector, so you can see at a glance the relationship between them.

Having completed the wheel, the person is encouraged to explore it. You can facilitate this process by asking questions such as:

- What did you notice from doing the wheel?
- Where are you in balance?
- Where are you out of balance?
- How satisfied are you with your current state of balance?
- Which wedges require immediate attention?
- How does X wedge impact on Y wedge?
- What action could change things?
- How would your life be different if you made a change leading you towards balance?

It is important to keep your questions neutral, or the coachee may get defensive. You will almost certainly have a number of thoughts and observations, but you'll want to keep them to yourself, so as to ensure the discussion remains focused on their agenda rather than on something that might be true for you. Especially avoid leading questions that take the conversation in a particular direction. Allow the discussion to continue until it comes to a natural close. By then both you and your client will have a much clearer idea of where they are, and possibly a strong idea of where they want to be.

Values Elicitation Process

Values are a crucial factor in the many choices we make every day. Many individuals, however, are unaware of their values until they're violated in some way, when an emotional reaction of some kind is likely to ensue. It is therefore valuable at the start of a coaching relationship to help people understand their value system. Asking some of the following questions will help elicit underlying values:

- What's important to you?
- What do you care about?
- What do you want more of in your life?
- What qualities do you really admire in people?
- When is life full and rich?

You can also find out what violates a value, and then turn it around to find the opposite by asking questions such as:

- What makes you angry?
- What qualities in people annoy you?
- What frustrates you?

Listen for 'shoulds' and 'oughts', which can indicate that the values are what the person believes would be the right kind of response to give. You might also find it useful to dig deeper if the answers appear superficial. If someone says that money is significant to them, you might ask what that gives them, to which they might reply 'freedom' – almost certainly a core value. Once the client has come up with a list of values, ask them to rank them in order of importance. Keep a note of the top three at least, because they will undoubtedly be impacting on the person's life in a major way. You can find out more about how values and beliefs can provide powerful levers for growth and development in Chapter 9.

Accountability

As part of the intake/discovery session, you will almost certainly want to talk with your client about how they would like you to 'hold them accountable' for things they say they would like to do. A common arrangement is for the coach to 'check in' the following week to find out how the client has been getting on with goals they set themself. In modern coaching practice, it's considered to be the responsibility of the client to make things happen, not the coach. If the client doesn't follow through, the coach's role is to explore the situation with them.

In a company context, when you're coaching your own staff, accountability is an area of potential conflict. Since you're putting in the time and effort to coach someone, you might feel the least they can do is follow through on the things they said they'd do. But if you start pressurizing them or seem unhappy when nothing has progressed, you risk the whole coaching relationship, as people may start to 'rebel', and avoid committing to anything they don't have to. Of course, it would be naive to suggest that a company arranging in-house coaching or employing the services of an external coach was not looking for some kind of 'improvement', but the best way of achieving it is by creating an environment in which people want to change, rather that trying to force them.

When you're not the right coach

Finally, you will want to ask yourself, 'Am I the right coach for this person?' You need to be scrupulously honest when addressing this issue. If you have any doubts about your competence or suitability, you should talk them through with the coachee. In *Coaching – Evoking Excellence in Others*, James Flaherty puts it this way: 'You don't have to have "chemistry" with your client. You don't have to be best friends or dinner companions, but you must have a workable relationship to fulfil your coaching work.'

As an independent you have some degree of control over whom you choose to coach. If you discover the relationship isn't working you have the option of not continuing, in which case the best thing you can do is give names and contact details of other coaches you feel might be more suited. You don't really have any choice if you want to regard yourself as a professional. You have a responsibility to do what is right for the client. And in the long run, operating with honesty, integrity and congruence will serve you well, as you gain a reputation as someone who coaches from the highest principles, not just for cash.

Things get more complicated when you have an arrangement with a company to coach several people. To say that it's not working with one member may risk putting the whole of the contract in jeopardy. You could bring in another coach suitable for the coachee, paid for out of the income you are receiving from the company. Once again, it's important to put the client's needs first, not your own.

If you're a coaching manager, and the relationship is not working, there may be wider issues that need to be addressed, and you may wish to speak to your human resources department. One alternative is to arrange peer coaching.

Primary focus

Having completed the intake/exploratory session most people are buzzing with ideas about what they want to do. Some will have come to coaching with one or more issues they would like to work with, but if not, doing the wheel will almost certainly have highlighted an area that stands out to them as a priority – and this will become the 'primary focus' for coaching. If there's time, you may get started on it straight away, during the first meeting you have together. If not, it can be picked up the next time you talk. Sometimes the person wants to work with that issue for several sessions, sometimes it's done in one. Occasionally they want to put it on pause, and return to it later. Once the primary focus has run its course, another issue takes its place as the one to be discussed. Over the course of a coaching relationship, many different areas are often covered, sometimes in parallel.

Outcome frame

It is important when working on an issue with your coachee that you encourage them to have an 'outcome frame' rather than a 'problem frame'. That is, rather than thinking about what's not working, what's wrong, or what they don't like, their attention is directed towards the future, towards the outcome they desire. One option is to take them through the SPACES process (see Chapter 3) as different issues come to the fore. Working this way over a period of time will give your coachee quite literally the opportunity to design their own life.

Anticipating setbacks

It's rare that a coaching relationship is one long string of successes, with each high point eclipsed by an even higher one the week after. Your clients are only human, they get disappointed, frustrated, dispirited. However, if you discuss this with them in the first session, they are much more likely to be able to take setbacks in their stride. This can also be a good time to raise the issue of the inner 'saboteur' which can get in the way of achieving what we want. Learning how to deal with it, or work round it, makes effecting personal change much easier. By making people aware of their 'saboteur', you can support them in noticing when it's influencing the situation adversely.

STRETCHING GOALS

Clients differ in the goals they set for themselves. Some reach for the stars, some their fingertips. As a coach, you can use your detached perspective to help them stretch. For most people that means setting incremental goals, each just a shade further than where they are right now. Not taking them too far outside their comfort zone, where they feel unsafe and can't function effectively, means they make solid, steady progress.

It is important, though, to be aware that such goals will not motivate everyone. Some people need more challenge than that, and when your client fits into that category you can encourage them to come up with goals that really stretch them. A skilled coach can help someone aspire to what others might consider an impossible goal – by relating it to their values, beliefs and highest aspirations.

COMPLETION

External coaches often agree with their clients a set number of coaching sessions over a defined period. At the outset they'll usually explain that the last session will be set aside for completion.

The final session isn't necessarily as final as it sounds. It's an opportunity either to re-contract with the client for further coaching sessions or to bring the relationship to a close. What it does do is to introduce an end point which gives the client the chance to take stock. Part of this 'stocktake' involves looking back over the course of the coaching relationship and using the review process to help the client integrate their learning at a conscious level. It's about consolidation and celebration. It gives them the chance to update their sense of self. If you keep effective notes during the coaching period you'll be able to refer back to the things they wanted to achieve and remind them of how much they've grown.

If you are an internal coach it's just as important to provide this opportunity to summarize your client's progress and to make sure they are ready for the next stage of their journey.

CHAPTER 8

Better Skills

To effectively communicate, we must realize that we are all different in the way we perceive the world and use this understanding as a guide to our communication with others.

ANTHONY ROBBINS

I listen a lot and talk less. You can't learn anything while you're talking.

BING CROSBY

TRUST

Trust is fundamental to effective coaching. Without it, the potential for growth and change is greatly diminished, and may even be destroyed entirely. Establishing trust is first and foremost about creating a 'safe space' which supports open communication – allowing the person to feel completely supported and sufficiently confident to open up about themself. There is unconditional acceptance of who they are, and no judgement of what they do or what they say.

Fostering trust is about being real, authentic, human and congruent. One way to achieve it is by admitting you don't have all the answers. This will help your clients to feel comfortable in setting aside their need to 'look good' and be willing to risk vulnerability. Your assurance of total confidentiality will encourage them to speak freely and honestly.

Trust goes hand-in-hand with believing that people are capable of achieving far more than they sometimes think they can. It's about being comfortable with not knowing the direction the client will take and trusting that whatever they choose will be right for them.

RAPPORT WORKS

Another way in which trust is created is through rapport – a fundamental part of effective communication and a vital component to building and maintaining effective relationships with other people. Rapport is something which happens naturally when two people feel at ease with each other. We often establish rapport with those who show interest in us and what we're doing or who demonstrate a real understanding of how we see the world. When two people are in rapport they naturally adapt their communications to suit the other person, and may alter their body language and the manner in which they speak accordingly.

People frequently think of rapport as something that can't be learnt, but there are numerous ways you can use it to enhance your skills as a coach. The starting point is to pay attention to aspects of your clients' behaviour which are normally outside your conscious awareness.

Progress now

The next time you're having a chat with a friend or a member of your family, make a mental note of as many things as possible you can observe about the way they use their body when interacting. Be aware of such things as:

- Whether they sit still or move their body position
- If they seem tense or relaxed
- Position of body (squared to other or sideways)
- Whether their head is tipped to one side or upright
- How the legs are positioned (flat on floor, crossed etc.)
- Movement of chest from breathing
- What kinds of hand gestures they make
- Whether they nod or shake their head
- If they're leaning back, upright or leaning forward
- Any expressions of the face (smiles/frowns, raised eyebrows etc.)

Notice also whether the movements change frequently during the course of an interaction, and whether gestures often punctuate and accentuate spoken communications.

HOW TO IMPROVE YOUR RAPPORT SKILLS

One simple way to enhance rapport is to match some aspect of your client's behaviour, such as the way they position their legs or move their arms or head. Be careful not to take this too far. If they notice what you're doing they will think you are mimicking them, and every last shred of rapport will be wiped out. The secret is subtlety. If you take matching to the extreme it will come across to your client as false and even manipulative. One way round this is to match what they do with another part of your body, for example, nodding your head in time with their tapping foot.

TELEPHONE COACHING

Coaches who provide telephone coaching have only the person's voice to work with. Fortunately it is still possible to establish rapport when working this way. As ever, the starting point is to notice what's going on. Because the visual element is missing, hearing becomes more finely tuned.

Matching the speed, volume and rhythm with which someone speaks will enhance rapport – and mismatching it will certainly break it.

It is also possible to pick up on the emotions of the speaker, although you must take care not to assume you know what they're feeling. All you are really doing is guessing, and when you start to make images in your mind or talk to yourself inside, you're not paying full attention to your client. When this happens, instead of saying something like, 'You seem anxious', you could say, 'I hear a tremor in your voice – what's going on for you right now?'

EXPERIENCE IS REVEALED BY LANGUAGE

Our deeper experience is revealed in our language whenever we speak, and another way of gaining rapport is to match the patterns in the words people use. Some of these patterns will be revealed by simply focusing your attention on the five senses. We take in information through our senses: visual (seeing), auditory (hearing), kinaesthetic (feeling), olfactory (smell) and gustatory (taste). When we think about something we re-experience it and then re-present the experience both verbally and non-verbally. The sense we prefer to use is reflected, among other things, in our choice of words, the way we breathe, and how we move our eyes.

Here are a few of the words most commonly used by people who favour visual, auditory or kinaesthetic language.

Visual	Auditory	Kinaesthetic
see	hear	feel
picture	mention	grab
focus	sound	hold

Visual	Auditory	Kinaesthetic
illustrate	wavelength	foundation
spot	attend	connect
clear	listen	put
look	say	touch
hazy	shout	cool
notice	loud	heated
glimpse	tune	handle
hindsight	voice	impact
view	call	tap
perspective	earful	foundation

Progress now

Start building your ability to spot the language people use by tuning into discussion programmes on the radio. This will give you lots of material to work with and no visual element to distract you.

Matching language patterns

Example of poor matching

Client: I sometimes feel quite intimidated by him. Almost like a little girl in his presence. Whereas most of the time, with my team or the other heads of department, I feel very different.

Coach: What sort of things does he say to you?

Client: (Pauses) Well, it isn't really about anything specific that he says. . . .

Example of good matching

Client: I sometimes feel quite intimidated by him. Almost like a little girl in his presence. Whereas most of the time, with my team or the other heads of department, I feel very different.

Coach: How specifically do you feel different?

Client: Well, I suppose I feel more like myself. I feel confident and purposeful. Whereas when I am sitting in front of his big desk I seem to shrink in size and I have this uneasy feeling in the pit of my stomach.

Coach: What stops you feeling confident?

In this second example the language used by both the client and coach is largely kinaesthetic – with most of the words used relating to feelings or emotions. In the first example the coach responds using auditory language and the question posed does not appear to fit the client's experience.

Non-verbal signals

It is possible to tell which sensory representation system a person is using simply by observing their eye movements. The table opposite lists the direction of eye movement of most people. A reversed pattern will usually be observed in a left-handed-person.

Visual construct – seeing internally things they have never seen before: Eyes up to the left

Visual recall – seeing internally things they have seen before: Eyes up to the right

Auditory construct – hearing words or sounds in a way they haven't heard them before: Eyes across to the left

Auditory recall – hearing words or sounds in a familiar way: Eyes across to the right

Kinaesthetic – feelings, emotions Down to the left

Auditory internal dialogue – talking to yourself Down to the right

Eye accessing cues

Progress now

Ask someone you know, 'What colour is your front door?' and watch their eyes. Then ask them to think of something that doesn't exist – such as a bright pink dog. Where are they looking now?

When you're coaching, being aware of these eye movements will not only help you build and maintain rapport but can also assist you in bringing about a shift in the other person by matching their reality. For example, if your client is deep into their feelings and emotions relating to an event that has taken place, you can either make a feelings-related enquiry to find out more or ask a question that gets them to look up and see the bright future ahead of them.

WHAT ELSE CAN WE LEARN ABOUT LANGUAGE?

Selective language

There's a wealth of information all around us every day. To avoid sensory overload our brains are selective about the amount we pay attention to. This shows up in the way we use language. We often 'delete' things by not referring to them or being specific about what we mean. When you are coaching it can be useful to gather the missing information. For example, if a client says, 'I want to make a good impression', you might ask, 'Who do you want to impress?' and 'How do you want to impress them?'

There are many different ways we 'delete' information. When you notice that information is missing ask where, when, what, how and who questions followed by 'exactly', 'specifically' or 'precisely'. You will find you have a better understanding about what's taking place and your client will gain clarity too. Take care though. This approach can annoy if you get the tone wrong. Aim for curiosity rather than interrogation. Your intention should be to support rather than intimidate your client.

Distortion

We also create our view of the world based on all the experiences we've had, the connections we've made to things, and how those things fit with our beliefs and values. Everyone's view is different. The problem is that we imagine others think the same as we do when that's often not the case. Our version of events is true for us – and as a result what we hear people say, is to some extent, a distortion. Being aware of this fact allows you to clarify your client's communication.

Mind reading

One common way things get distorted is through 'mind reading' – by having meaning attributed to them. You might believe, for example, that a colleague won't like what you're planning based either on your past experience of their reaction or because you wouldn't like it if you were in their position. But you are really guessing. You won't know until you talk to them about it. So if you have a client who says, 'My assistant isn't going to like this' you can respond with, 'It sounds like you're mind reading. What steps could you take to find out for certain how he feels about it?'

When you're coaching it's easy to fall into the mind reading trap. If you have personal experience of a situation similar to one your client brings up it can be tempting to imagine they're the same. You are then in danger of suggesting a solution rather than following your client's thread.

Bounded thinking

We naturally look for patterns and connections between things. Our brains categorize all the information we take in and we later draw upon these pools of knowledge in a general rather than specific fashion. This way of processing information limits our thinking as we create boundaries around what we believe is possible based on our generalized experience.

Being aware of this allows you as coach to help your client to expand the limits they have placed on their world. For example, a client might say, 'I can't speak to my boss', to which a useful reply would be, 'What would happen if you did?' This makes the client imagine what it will be like to talk with their boss and opens up a new way of thinking about the situation. This type of question can also bring to the surface the beliefs a client holds that are limiting the number of options available to them.

FOCUS OF ATTENTION

People tend to excel when they're focused on the task in hand. Coaching is no different, only in this case your attention is focused on your client. During a session it's important to be aware of the times when your focus drifts to your inner world. When this happens you will start to lose rapport and stop noticing what's going on. You need to get back in flow.

Chapter 4 described how interference can get in the way of achievement. When you are fully connected with what you are doing, all self-talk disappears. To get back in flow it's simply a matter of switching your focus of attention and turning off the interference. Over time, maintaining your attention becomes a skill that works at the level of unconscious competence. It can operate in the same way that you learn to become aware of body language and after a while you no longer have to think about it consciously.

Tips for building your listening skills

- Stop talking – you can't speak and listen. Some of your best coaching sessions will be those when you say hardly anything at all.

- Be careful not to interrupt especially when you think your client may not have understood your question.
- Show you're listening. Your body language will show if you're attending.
- Suspend judgement. Let go of your opinion and focus on what your client feels is the best option
- Be patient – the meaning may become clear. Allow the client the space and time to think things through out loud.
- Become more aware of your internal voice. Your inner voice will divert your attention from the client. When this happens follow the client's train of thought instead of your own, and trust that you will know exactly what to say when and if the appropriate time arises.
- Listen for what's not said. Listen for patterns in what your client says and in what they don't say. When you bring one of these patterns to your client's attention they may or may not make a connection with what you are saying. Whatever happens, accept it – as another avenue explored.

As a coach you'll find yourself listening for patterns in what your client says and in what they don't say. When you observe one of these patterns you sometimes want to say it out loud to your client – to introduce it as something you've noticed. Then let go of being right. The client will either make a connection with what you are saying or it may lead nowhere. Whatever happens, it will be another avenue explored.

Everyone can benefit from enhancing their listening skills and the rewards are well worth the effort involved. Listening can take place at different levels. The basic level of listening is where we hear what's said and then reflect on what it means to us. This is great for taking in information but not so useful when you're coaching. If you're listening in this way it's likely that you'll be tempted to start giving advice based on your own experience.

When your attention is fully focused on the other person you'll find that you're aware of not only the words they say but the expressions they use. The quality of your coaching depends on how well you listen. Some of the best coaches around have developed almost a sixth sense when they're listening.

Progress now

Over the next few weeks monitor how well you are listening. Enlist the help of someone you trust to give you feedback on how you're doing. Make a tape recording of a coaching session – after getting permission from the client. When you play it back, note the quality of your listening.

WHAT MAKES A QUESTION POWERFUL?

In some ways there's no such thing as a powerful question. Often it's the simplest question asked at the right time that's effective in moving a client forward. More often than not a 'powerful' question will be followed by a brief silence, as the client disappears down a path of discovery. Every new direction opens up further possibilities, adds to the client's understanding of themself and creates options for them so they can take another step towards achieving their goals.

Different question words elicit different types of response – the client will interpret whatever you ask in a way that fits their reality. Enquiries starting with 'why' can be experienced as accusatorial, and often result in justification or defence. For that reason they are best avoided. A better option would be, 'What was happening there?'. Similarly, questions that require a factual response or a simple yes or no are more likely to narrow thinking than expand it.

Types of Question

- **Closed.** Requires a short and usually factual answer and often brings discussion to a halt. Instead of, 'Is this the best way forward for you?' you could ask, 'What's the best way forward for you?'
- **Open**. Encourages the other person to provide an expansive answer. 'What other choices could you make?'
- **Encouraging**. Lets the other person know you're interested. 'What else happened?'
- **Probing**. Gets the other person to expand on their comments, or encourages them to look at things in greater depth. 'What do you think they meant by that?'
- **Reflective.** Reflects back something implied by what someone has said. 'So you feel valued?'

- **Clarification.** Provides a summary of what's been said in order to check that you've fully understood. 'Am I right in saying that you believe . . . ?'
- **Hypothetical.** Encourages people to think more creatively and generate new options. 'If you could get round that problem, what would you do?'
- **Leading**. States the required response in the question, so people will tend to give you the answer you want, whether or not it represents their view. If you say, 'Don't you think it would be better to do it this way?', you are implying they are wrong and you are right. Avoid using these.

Powerful coaching questions

What do you want?

What will you have to do to complete this?

What stops you?

What's the real issue here?

How does this fit with your values?

What's the learning from this?

What action can you take?

What is important to you?

How could you think of this as easy?

What are you unwilling to confront?

Where do you go from here?

How might this translate into action?

What form might that take?

What would qualify as a significant step?

What else?

What next?

What options do you have?

How will it feel to have mastered this?

What other perspectives could you have?

What's obvious here?

What would be the perfect question to ask you right now?

A question is only powerful if it comes at the right moment – the 'dumbest' questions can be the most effective.

USING THE GROW MODEL

The GROW model (introduced in Chapter 2) can be used to practise questioning skills. For example:

Goal What do you want?
What will it be like when you've achieved it?
Imagine you have reached your goal right now. What does it look, sound and feel like?

Reality Tell me about your current situation.
What, specifically, is happening right now?
What's holding you back?

Options What else could you consider?
What are the pros and cons of . . .?
What other options are there?

What next What steps will you take next?
What might stop you?
When we speak in two weeks time, what will you tell me?

THE POWER OF SILENCE

One of the most useful things a coach can learn is to become comfortable with silence. Once you start to ask powerful questions you'll find your clients take time to answer. There can be a temptation to fill the void or explain your question – and this breaks the other person's train of thought. The key is to trust that the client will come up with something, even if it's, 'I don't know'. A great follow-up question to this is, 'And if you did know' or, 'Just guess.' The client's unconscious mind knows more than they are aware of and these types of questions often open up new channels of thought.

INCREASING CHOICE

Questions open up new possibilities, and coaching is fundamentally about extending the number of options your client has available, of fostering autonomy.

Some people attribute responsibility for things that happen in their lives to other people. You often hear it in the language they use. When someone says, 'He makes me feel angry' they are 'ducking out' and blaming the other person for how they feel. As a coach you can encourage your client to recognize these patterns. A useful question you might ask is, 'How does his behaviour mean you feel angry?', which allows the client to consider other emotional choices.

It can be tempting to commiserate with your client by identifying with the problem they're presenting. When you do this you're reinforcing the client's view that the situation cannot be changed. There's a big difference between empathy and sympathy. Empathy allows you to identify with the other person. For a coach to say, 'I can tell you feel confused about this' is very different from saying, 'Yes, that is confusing'. The latter statement implies they can't change it. The former acknowledges the situation but leaves it more open, ready for the next step towards achieving clarity.

Another fundamental skill of coaching is 'not knowing'. The answers do not lie within the coach, and a key part of the coach's role is about making room for the client to feel safe to explore their world. It's about trusting the client to find the right solution for themself from within. The less you teach the more they learn.

Corporate culture

The culture in many organizations demands that bosses know the answers. In some organizations effort is made to reverse this trend and managers often say they would like their team members to be more self-reliant and to come to them with a solution rather than a problem. Coaching can provide some clues here of what stops this from happening. The first step for the manager is to move out of the way and create some space for the team to develop their ideas of how to make progress.

How not to offer a solution

- **Deal with your internal dialogue.** The more you become aware of the conversations you have with yourself while you are coaching the more you can put them to one side and concentrate on 'not knowing'.
- **Practise being really present.** Give your clients your full attention.
- **Enter their world.** Focus on what it means to them.
- **Aim to create space.** Detach yourself from any particular outcome and in the process become more available to your client.
- **Adopt a curious frame of mind.** Resist the temptation to relate what others say to your own experience.
- **You don't need the answers.** Remind yourself that every time a client comes up with a solution they are also building confidence in their own ability to solve their problems. They grow as a result and your restraint has aided them in that process.
- **Let go of solutions.** If you want to offer an option, ask permission first. You risk frustrating the client if you appear to be unwilling to share their own experience.
- **Keep at it.** Not offering a solution is a skill that needs practice like any other.

SKILLS THAT HELP TO STRETCH CLIENTS

One of the ways you can help a client move forward is by holding a client accountable for what they commit to doing. As a coach you can help them make sure their goal is realistic or suggest they report back to you when they've completed it. They must feel free to change their minds, though. In doing so they may even learn something about themselves, their values or their sense of identity. This may lead them in a new direction that feels right for them.

Your aim is to 'hold your clients big' rather than 'keep them small'. In practice this means believing in their potential to achieve what they set out to do and matching this belief in the words that you use. Consider the difference between these two questions.

- Can you recall a time when a presentation you delivered went really well?
- Tell me about a time when you delivered a presentation really well.

The first question implies doubt in their ability to find such a memory and 'keeps them small'. The second suggests they'll be able to find an answer to your question and 'holds them big'. The key is to see the potential not just the person as they appear to you now.

When a client is making good progress with their goals you can offer them a challenge. The key to success lies in making sure what you're asking them to do is in their best interest. You're aiming stretch them a little further. By doing this you're also implying that you believe they're capable of achieving it.

Another skill of coaching is acknowledging. This is all about recognizing the person rather than a behaviour or action. It's about making an observation about your client that rings true for them – they recognize themself. A coach might say, 'You were strong and followed it through'. This is different from offering praise: 'Good job, well done'. Praise implies the coach has given approval and this is more likely to result in dependency. Acknowledgement supports the client and reinforces their self-belief.

CHAPTER 9

Better Experience

The true meaning of life is to plant trees under whose shade you do not expect to sit.

NELSON HENDERSON

For a long time it had seemed to me that life was about to begin – Real Life. But there was always some obstacle in the way, something to be gotten through first. Then, life would begin. At last it dawned on me that these obstacles were my life.

ALFRED D. SOUZA

BEING FLEXIBLE AS A COACH

A coach needs to be flexible in order to be effective. If you tackle every individual in exactly the same way, a lot of the time you are not going to be effective.

The starting point to being a flexible coach is to observe the client – not just their body language but their whole demeanour and attitude too. Gather information not just in terms of what they say and do, but also relating to their sense of what's right, who they are, and what they want.

Being aware of the person in front of you as a unique individual means you will tailor your coaching accordingly. This means being sensitive to the person's 'map' of reality, and coaching in a way that makes it as easy as possible to establish and maintain rapport – so they achieve what they want.

It's also essential to be aware that people change over time, even from week to week. Make sure you keep up with any changes they've made. It's all too easy to operate on the basis of an outdated perspective.

CASE STUDY

BEING FLEXIBLE

In two coaching sessions, which ran straight after each other, the coach found it necessary to adapt his approach to meet the different needs of the clients. The first session was with a quiet, relatively introverted woman who liked to take time to think things through. It was her first experience of being coached, and the coach needed to provide lots of questions to keep things moving forward. The second session was with someone who was extremely self-aware, had done lots of self-development work, and worked as a coach himself. Because he 'processed' quickly, and often took the next step himself, the coach needed only to ask a searching question now and again and then provide a gentle nudge here and there. To do more would have been experienced as intrusive.

RESISTANCE TO COACHING

Individuals who approach a life coach on their own behalf can normally be expected to be enthusiastic participants in the process. In a corporate setting, however, people might be reluctant to have coaching for various reasons, including

- Associating coaching with underperformance
- Not being willing to accept there is room for improvement
- Mistrust of the motives of the organization
- Not wanting to look at themself
- Fear of change
- Not wanting to be coached by you (position power, past experiences)
- Happy as they are
- Not wanting to go outside their comfort zone
- Fear of failure
- Company culture getting in the way

If the person admits to their resistance, you are in a position to acknowledge their concerns and to discuss them. You then have a dialogue going which can form the basis of an ongoing relationship.

Sometimes, though, the resistance is 'passive': people are uncooperative and contribute nothing to proceedings. When you can't overcome this barrier, the best thing may be to suggest another coach – especially where you suspect that there is a lack of trust. Often when you discuss this with them you get the breakthrough you're looking for.

WHEN THE CLIENT GETS STUCK

After the first few sessions, a client may find they're not making as much progress as they'd like, that they are repeating patterns that have held them back in the past.

When people find themselves stuck, the most important thing is to get them to stay with the process, and to become more aware of their patterns of behaviour and thinking. You can assist by giving feedback on what you see, hear and feel, and add value by attending to ways in which your client appears to be limiting themself in their thinking. Pay attention in particular to words such as 'can't', 'should', 'ought', 'must' and 'need', which indicate unwritten rules that may be underpinning their behaviour. By bringing them to conscious attention, and challenging them, the person can begin to make more appropriate choices.

Sometimes these patterns are deep, and derive from significant emotional events in the person's past. If so, it may be beyond your ability, and indeed responsibility, as a coach to deal with them, and therapy or counselling may be more appropriate.

Work problems often mask personal issues and vice versa, and to be effective, coaching needs to address the whole of the client's life. Issues that show up in the work situation often have parallels elsewhere.

ON THE LEVEL

One approach that can be useful when people get stuck is the hierarchy of neurological levels devised by anthropologist Gregory Bateson and popularized by Robert Dilts. Drawing on research about the way humans process information, it is a framework that can assist you in thinking about change and personal development. It consists of six levels of meaning at which a person can be operating or where they might be stuck.

1. **Environment – where and when things are done.** This can be a physical environment, such as a building, or a more abstract environment, such as the culture of an organization. At this level you can explore the restrictions, limitations and opportunities the environment may present for your client.

2. **Behaviour – what is done.** The actual behaviour involved, which can be an action or a reaction. Coaching at this level is often about desired versus actual behaviour.

3. **Capabilities – how we think and how things are done.** This level relates to knowledge, skills, processes, strategies and plans. What we perceive is translated into a direction to be taken. At this level you explore the thinking underpinning your client's behaviour.

4. **Beliefs and values – why things are done.** This can be a rich area to explore when you're coaching as this is often the level where people place limits on what it is possible for them to achieve. You're seeking to help them find ways of giving themselves permission to do things.
5. **Identity – who am I?** Who someone thinks they are – their sense of self, their role. This is more abstract than beliefs: it is where the things we've experienced have shaped us at a deep level into who we are. Every day, experience subtly changes who we are.
6. **Spirituality/vision – For whom or what?** This is about how we influence the larger system surrounding us of which we are a part and how that system shapes and changes us. When you're coaching someone who is clear about their purpose you'll often find them energized and aligned with what they want.

The higher the level of the hierarchy, the greater the leverage for change. Many people get stuck at levels 2 and 3 – 'I can't X' or 'I'll never be able to Y'. While it is possible to tackle the issues at those levels, you are likely to be more effective if you work at the next level up. When the issue is about capabilities (level 3), the best level to go in at is often beliefs (level 4): challenge and update your client's beliefs.

The neurological levels make a useful diagnostic tool, enabling you to detect the level at which someone is stuck by the language they use. Consider the sentence: 'I can't do that here'. Each word represents a level.

I	Identity
Can't	Beliefs
Do	Capabilities
That	Behaviour
Here	Environment

If the emphasis is placed on 'here' it may be that the organization the person works for is the issue. It's important to be careful not to make assumptions, though, as the real stumbling block could be the individual's *beliefs* about what the organization will allow them to do rather than a reality.

The most profound changes can be leveraged by getting people to consider their issues from their sense of who they are and why they are here – the identity or spirituality/vision levels. Problems which seemed overwhelming and insurmountable can often seem as nothing when viewed from such a perspective.

DIFFERENT PERSPECTIVES

Another process that's valuable for opening up your client's world involves getting them to see things from different points of view. First, though, it may be useful to reflect on how we perceive the world. Generally we are looking out from our own perspective at other people and things. This is called first position in neuro linguistic programming (NLP) terminology. We can only be aware of what our senses take in and we automatically filter external data with little or no conscious input – we associate what we are experiencing through our senses with information that has been accumulating in our memories since the day we were born.

This first perceptual position stays with us throughout life and is important in that it helps us to make sense of the information we take in through our senses. It also allows us to value our own needs. When used in isolation, however, it can be very limiting – and can distance us from other people and their needs.

The act of mentally stepping into someone else's shoes allows you to adopt a different perspective. By doing this you start to be able to picture the world from their point of view. The more you are able to do this, the more it increases your awareness of what they intend to accomplish by their words and actions.

In coaching you'll often find that your client is experiencing difficulty with another person's behaviour. If, for example, they feel let down by someone close to them, who perhaps did not complete a task they promised to do, it would be helpful for them to be able to identify that person's positive intent. Perhaps by not completing the task this person could conceal their lack of knowledge. Their intent might be to 'feel safe' and this may have driven them to hide behind unacceptable behaviour.

Stepping into someone else's shoes can be useful as it allows us to accept and understand the other person as an individual rather than just focusing on their behaviour. While you can't change anyone else – only they can do that – you can change how you behave towards them. By detaching yourself from the situation and acting like an observer you gain a clear view of the situation. From this position you can consider future possibilities. Once you've identified a change you can try it out and see, hear and feel the difference it makes on how you feel about the other person. In the above example this person could be helped by our creating an environment where they could feel safe to make mistakes as they learn.

Progress now

This exercise can be used to improve any relationship and you can either use it with a client or take aspects of the exercise to expand their thinking about their relationship with another person. It involves taking up three positions: (1) you, (2) the other person, (3) a dissociated position.

Starting in the first position, picture the person you want to have a better relationship with. Tune in to what they might say to you. See the look on their face when they look at you. Get in touch with how you feel.

Break your emotional state in some way to release any emotion attached to this person or situation. This can be as simple as distracting your attention by thinking about something different for a few moments.

Next, step into the shoes of this other person – be them. What do you see through their eyes? What do you hear? What do you feel? What is the positive intention behind this behaviour?

Once again break your emotional state to release the emotions attached to this person.

Move now into the third position and notice how you respond to the you in first position. What can you learn that may be useful to you? What changes do you want to make to the way you respond to this person?

Take this learning back to first position and try it out. Notice how the look on the other person's face may have changed in response to this change in you. Hear the difference in the tone of their voice as they respond to you. Be aware of the difference in the way you feel inside.

The more times you repeat these stages the more insights you're likely to get giving you more options of how to respond to their behaviour.

CHANGING PERSPECTIVES

Chris wanted to improve his relationship with his boss. Whenever he suggested new ideas or a specific approach to take with a customer, his boss seemed to dismiss what he said without giving the idea a chance. This left him feeling his suggestions were not valued; his judgement seemed to be in question and this was starting to affect his self-esteem. The coach asked Chris to imagine being his boss and then to listen to him (the client) explain a new idea. Chris went away to think about this and at the next session took delight in explaining how he had a new strategy to use with his boss in these situations. When he put himself in the position of his boss Chris realized he didn't explain the thinking process behind his ideas and that his boss just wanted to feel confident that the idea would work. A small change in Chris's behaviour brought about a big improvement in his relationship with his boss.

UTILIZING METAPHOR

People use metaphorical language all the time to enrich and extend the meaning of what they say. A client may introduce a metaphor to describe an obstacle they're facing or to express how they feel about something. A common one is, 'I feel like I'm hitting a brick wall.' Picking up on the metaphor, the coach can respond, 'Tell me more about the brick wall.' Some clients will continue by describing the features of the wall, its height or the colour of the bricks or stone it is made from. Metaphor gets past the conscious, analytical part of our minds and goes deeper into our inner experience. Getting your clients to articulate their metaphors can be a useful way of understanding how they make sense of their lives.

On occasions the opportunity may present itself to you to introduce a metaphor that illuminates your client's understanding of an issue. If someone is feeling impatient with the time it's taking for a project to get off the ground, a metaphor about putting down foundations before the building can go up or not digging up a seedling to see if the roots have grown might help provide a useful perspective.

CASE STUDY

SPINNING PLATES

Viv spoke a number of times to his coach about feeling out of control – unable to keep all his plates spinning without them crashing to the ground. Picking up on the metaphor, the coach asked Viv to consider various options to prevent that happening. One he'd never thought of was to put some of the plates down, so there were fewer to keep spinning. Transferring that realization into the real world, Viv let go of some the tasks he'd been trying unsuccessfully to tackle, and was able to devote more time to making the others work well.

USING INTUITION

Intuition can be valuable in coaching, but needs to be used with care. When your 'gut instinct' has served you well a number of times you'll begin to trust it more – although often what you say won't fit for the client. When you do express these thoughts to a client it's useful to let them know that's what you are doing. The client will then either accept what you've said, or may choose to reject it.

As a coach it's important that you let go of any attachment you have to your intuition. If it fits for the client, fine – if it doesn't that's fine too. In your coaching relationships you will also discover there's a fine line between speaking your intuition and raising issues that relate to what's going on for you – and it's important that over time you learn to recognize the difference between the two. Sometimes you'll get an intuition that makes no sense to you. If you say it anyway you may be surprised at how often it resonates with the client. They may even pick it up and work with it like a metaphor, interpreting it in a way that connects with their world.

DEVELOPING YOUR OWN STYLE

As you develop your coaching skills you'll be trying out lots of techniques and ideas to find out what works for you. What's most important is that your coaching style reflects your personality. Many people are rather serious when they start out because that's how they believe coaches are supposed to be. But, if you're naturally witty and playful, this earnestness can come across as false – and make your clients wary. Another important aspect of how you develop your coaching style relates to the way coaching fits with your sense of identity and purpose in life. If you are able to connect to what's really important to you, your coaching will start to come alive as you drop using techniques and start to communicate with clients at a deeper level.

Progress now

Write a list of ten words that best describe your personality, and another list of ten that describe how you are when coaching. If there's a discrepancy you might want to review your approach to coaching. What would happen if you allowed your real self to shine through?

COACHING AS A WAY OF BEING

As a coach, you don't just impact on one person. Everyone you coach interacts with many other people, and the ripples spread out, with the changes you support people in making also affecting many others you will never meet.

Because coaching has such a powerful impact on both individuals and the community at large, you might like to imagine what would happen if instead of regarding it as something you did every now and again, you were to adopt it as a way of being in the world – so that it was second nature, a part of the way you operate, part of who you are.

If you're a manager, one of the ways you can achieve this is to use coaching as your first option, not the last resort or only for special occasions. When someone asks for your help, or there is an acknowledged need for you to intervene, approach the problem as a coach by asking the person to give their own understanding of the situation and to come up with their own solutions. Resist the temptation to be the manager as expert, working hands-on to make sure things are done – and done right.

> 'The temptation for many managers is to slip back into a much more directional approach, particularly in difficult or pressurised situations,' says a report on coaching by the Industrial Society. 'Generally speaking, the longer a coach is non-directional, the more long-term learning will be achieved. Managers often think that part of their management role is about controlling people. This is a misconception, both because the highest performance comes from those who are empowered to make their own decisions, and because, with flatter structures and increasing numbers of direct reports, managers literally don't have the time or resources.'

Almost every question and complaint gives you an opportunity to coach your team. With you acting as a role model, team members soon learn to coach themselves. Over time they'll internalize the kinds of question you ask them and start to ask them of themselves and others before approaching you. You'll find they come up with the answer without needing to ask for your help, and you will have been saved time and avoided being distracted.

Making coaching a way of being means there'll be a constant focus on development and empowerment – not something that happens in discrete packages, at fixed times, by going on a course, or only within the context of a formal coaching session, but always present as an element in the day. Coaching in this way can play a part in creating a genuine learning organization, where people are encouraged to rely upon their own resources, supported by but not dependent on others.

COACHING TEAMS

It's a relatively small step from using your coaching skills with individuals to using a coaching approach when working with groups and teams. The principles are the same, but the scale and some of the practicalities are different. As ever, as coach you ask questions, encourage the team to set the agenda, and let them decide what action needs to be taken. Doing so can quickly facilitate open, honest communication channels and mutual trust.

Coaching can be appropriate for any team but, if the individuals are newly formed into a group and relatively inexperienced, you may opt for team building initially. Team coaching will often be very effective where the individuals have the experience and maturity to work autonomously. When you want to build cohesion, establish commitment to a common goal and engender team spirit, there's no better way of doing it than by coaching. Indeed, coaching has been shown to be particularly effective in self-managing teams with cross-functional responsibility, set up to tackle a specific task.

Potential rivalries, tensions, competing agendas and personality clashes between team members might become problematic without a firm hand on team coaching sessions. As ever, there is a need to 'design the alliance' properly in the first place – to establish ground rules on how things will operate. To maintain the team's autonomy it should be responsible for monitoring what's going on: surfacing and resolving any conflicts as they arise. Coaching a team is best done by someone other than the team's manager or leader.

You can of course combine team coaching with one-to-one sessions with each individual. A particular additional advantage of this is that people often open up more easily in a group setting when they've had the chance to do so with a coach one-on-one.

SELF-COACHING

All coaching is self-learning. You cannot make your clients grow or develop – nor should you try. All you can do is be a guide for them as they explore the options open to them. But you can help yourself to learn and grow – and you have a responsibility to do so, so that you are even more effective in the way you operate.

There are many ways of improving your coaching skills and an important one is to get feedback from your clients. This element is a feature of all the best training schools, as the only way you can really know how effective you are being is by direct report from those you work with. The feedback shapes and re-forms the alliance between you. That is why designing the alliance is meant to be an ongoing process not just something you do at the start and then forget about.

Progress now

Describe (1) what makes your coaching magical, and (2) what would make it even more magical.

The difference between the two is your 'growing edge', your opportunity to take your coaching to the next level. Focusing on this will mean you inevitably make the improvements you desire for yourself and your clients.

CHAPTER 10

Balancing Coaching with the Rest of your Life

Until you value yourself, you won't value time. Until you value time, you will not do anything with it.

M. SCOTT PECK

It's easy to say 'no!' when there's a deeper 'yes!' burning inside.

STEPHEN COVEY, ROGER MERRELL AND REBECCA MERRELL

USING THE WHEEL OF LIFE

The wheel of life (see page 160) can be used to consider the implications of a particular issue: in this case becoming a coach. The eight sectors of the wheel are labelled:

Career/Work; Partner/Spouse; Friends and Family; Money; Health and Fitness; Fun; Environment; and Personal Development.

Progress now

Create a Wheel of Life for yourself and mark each segment with a line to represent a number between 0 and 10 (0 being at the centre of the wheel and 10 being at the rim). How do you rate your current balance – or lack of it? Which segments are you happy with? Which, if any, would you like to change? And, specifically, how might your current equilibrium be affected as coaching becomes more important?

Career/Work

For managers planning to use their coaching skills with their teams it's likely to be Career/Work that will feel the greatest impact as coaching becomes more important.

If you focus on excelling at work by making coaching a priority, there may be less time for you to spend with your family. That may be the case initially, but over the mid to long term the opposite is usually the case. Because coaching ultimately allows people to grow their skills and confidence they are able to take on additional responsibility, giving them more, not less, time.

Those seeking a shift into working as an external coach will be faced with the challenge of getting the word out and building a client base. This can be a time-consuming business in the early stages. Taking on the extra time commitment to make your dream of earning your living as a coach become a reality can impact heavily on other areas of your life.

Partner/Spouse

The segment that often bears the brunt of an already excessive or increased workload is that of Partner/Spouse. In a recent survey, more than half of British workers said they would like to cut back on the hours they work, one of the main reasons being that the long hours were affecting their relationships.

As you contemplate investing more of your time in coaching, you will inevitably want to consider the implications for any close relationship. If time is tight already, a couple of extra hours spent coaching each week could be the straw that breaks the camel's back. If coaching is to be given priority, something else may have to give.

Friends and Family

As long as you organize things sensibly you won't see too much impact on this segment as a result of putting their coaching plans into practice.

Money

This segment of the wheel is closely tied to the Career/Work area of people's lives. Those aspiring to earn a living as a life coach or executive coach need to be aware that it can take some time to build up a business to the position where coaching can be your only source of income. In the meantime you will need either some other means of earning a living, preferably part-time, or a partner willing and able to support you through the early stages.

Health and Fitness

Whether you are a fitness fanatic or a couch potato, coaching is unlikely to change the way in which you prioritize this segment.

Fun

For many people running a coaching session can be extremely enjoyable. You *can* sit there with your client and be deadly earnest, but you are more likely to engage their interest and motivation if you have some fun along the way – and it's perfectly possible to do that without trivializing the practice of coaching or the issues with which your client is working.

Environment

Coaching is unlikely to have an immediate impact upon your home environment. If you coach inside an organization, finding private areas away from the workplace can be a challenge. A wider environmental issue relates to the organization's culture in which you are attempting to operate. How people perceive coaching and the benefits it brings can prove to be either an area of concern or something that aids the whole learning process.

Personal Development

One of the great things about coaching is that during every session you benefit from the insights of your clients – insights that often seem to have relevance to an issue with which you too are grappling.

Progress now

Identify something small that would help you achieve your goal. Whatever you choose will become part of your daily routine – a habit. Make the habit specific so you know if you've achieved it, such as spending 10 minutes a day reading a novel for fun.

Keep a record of each time you do your 'new habit' for at least a month. Writing down what you intend to do increases your commitment to it and checking your record of daily habits will keep you mindful of the commitments you have made to yourself. After about six weeks it's likely that your new habit will become part of your routine.

Don't forget to celebrate your success as this will encourage you to keep on going. To increase your chances of sticking to your plans, find a way to combine the habit with something you do already.

IF TIME WERE MADE OF ELASTIC

Managing time will often be an issue for the people you coach. As you discovered in Chapter 6, the progress we make with building our skills or attaining our goals is often incremental. We build our skills one step at a time, until we reach the point where we do things without even thinking about them: we develop habits. You can use this tendency to create routines to fit more of what you want into your life and feel comfortable rather than pressured by the things you want to achieve in the time you have available.

How do you spend your time?

We are often unaware of the ways in which we waste time – and with it our power and effectiveness. Simply finding out how you actually fill your days will give you valuable information that will enable you to make realistic decisions about managing your time better – letting go of the things you feel waste your time and begin to value each moment.

Progress now

Keep a note in your diary for at least a week on how you spend your time. Choose a period that is reasonably typical and record *everything* as you go along, say every hour or so.

The next stage is to look for patterns in the information you have gathered. How much time do you spend overall sleeping, working, travelling, having fun with the family, walking in the country or exercising? If you were to guess what was important to someone who spent their time the way that you do, what do you think it would be?

Looking at what receives the most attention will tell you where your priorities *really* lie. There is often a significant difference between the way you thought you were using your time and the way you actually do. If a particular area of your life is important to you but is getting neglected, consider the steps you can take to move it higher up your agenda. Now you know what has been happening you can choose to change.

BEING REALISTIC

Many people are unrealistic about time – they have more things they want to do than they have time for, and they end up making themselves stressed.

Make time for your life – secrets for success

1. **Start saying no to things you don't want to do.** If you like to please others you may find this a particularly useful area on which to focus. People won't be offended if you say no from time to time and they would often prefer that to having someone less than enthusiastic or with limited time to devote to the job.
2. **Understand your energy cycle.** Get a sense of when you feel most energetic and when you start to become more lethargic. Use your best times of the day for the things you find most difficult and the other time for routine things.
3. **Watch for the times when you procrastinate.** If it won't take long, do it now. If it's a larger project, break it down into small tasks and do short bursts on each one. That way it won't seem so daunting and your tendency to resist will be reduced. Reflect on the strategies you are using to hold back from completing things and use some of the ideas from Chapter 6 to install new ones.

4. **Reduce the number of meetings you go to.** Only attend those with a clear aim, relevant agenda and agreed time frame. Ask yourself how important the meeting really is. What would happen if you didn't attend?

5. **If you are a manager of a team, think about how you delegate.** If someone in your team can do a job 80% as well as you it's well worth giving them the chance to develop their skills. First analyse the task. Can you delegate it? Next analyse the people. Do they have the right skills? Will they be able to do the task with training? What is their current workload like? What are your own feelings about the task? What, if anything, stops you letting go of it? Once you've decided to delegate it, devise a monitoring system that ensures it will go smoothly for them and for you.

6. **Clear out your clutter and get organized.** Set up good systems to streamline everyday tasks. Take a look at your desk. If you can see less than 80% of it then it is likely that working this way is adding to your stress levels and you could be wasting time searching for things.

7. **Look after yourself.** Take regular mini-breaks at work, drink lots of water, look after your diet and take time for stress-releasing activities like going to the gym, yoga or meditation.

CHAPTER 11

To Boldly Go!

Whatever you can do. Or dream you can. Begin it. Boldness has genius, power and magic in it. Begin it now.

GOETHE

If a person is living out his destiny, he knows everything he needs to know.

PAUL COELHO

Dance like no one is watching,
Love like you will never be hurt,
Sing like no one is listening,
Live like it's heaven on earth.

WILLIAM PURKEY

WHAT IS YOUR QUEST?

The act of coaching other people will clearly help you to continue to develop your skills but, when you work alone, it can be easy to fall into a routine way of going about things. Some coaches find they have an unconscious tendency to ask questions around a particular need they personally have when they get stuck or want to solve a problem. It's as if they're on their own quest in search of a solution. A similar thing can occur when your client's issue reminds you of a previous client or triggers something about your own life experience. In these situations you need to catch yourself doing it quickly and make sure you follow your client's thinking process rather than your own.

Progress now

Reflect on some of the coaching you have done. What patterns do you observe in the sorts of questions you ask?

YOU AND YOUR SHADOW

No matter how skilled you are as a coach, you will almost certainly encounter people who create an extra challenge for you. Maybe you just don't hit it off but you can't put your finger on why, or perhaps there's a particular behaviour or characteristic that upsets or bothers you. If these attributes are different each time, then it's possible they are a true reflection of the individual. But if there's a pattern, with the same issues coming up repeatedly, it makes sense to ask whether the common denominator is you. One possibility is that you are 'projecting' on to your client aspects of your 'shadow', with the result that your experience of them is distorted.

The 'shadow' is a term that derives from the work of Carl Jung, and describes those parts of ourselves we dislike and disown, and which have been repressed from consciousness. They are often the opposite of what we regard as our 'positive' attributes, and formed our shadow during the course of our childhood as we developed our personality, and decided who we are and who we are not. So if we think of ourselves as clever, approachable, efficient and loyal, our shadow side – those characteristics which we are not comfortable expressing because they do not fit with our sense of identity – will include stupid, unapproachable, inefficient and disloyal. But repression does not eliminate these qualities or stop them from functioning, it merely removes them from consciousness awareness. Sometimes they form a part of our personality we ourselves cannot see but which is readily observable by others.

To make ourselves feel better about this 'dark' side of our nature, we unconsciously project the attributes we have repressed on to others.

> When we react intensely to a quality in an individual or group and our reaction overtakes us with great loathing or admiration this may be our own shadow showing. We project by attributing this quality to the other person in an unconscious effort to banish it from ourselves.'
>
> Connie Zweig and Jeremiah Abrams

So if we have a side to our character which is impatient, but we are unaware of it, and we think of ourselves as patient, then we may find ourselves noticing, commenting on and being annoyed by what we see as impatient behaviour in others.

An awareness of the shadow is important because it can easily interfere with your effectiveness as a coach. Once you become aware of what is in your shadow you can do something about it – sometimes it is enough simply to acknowledge the repressed characteristics in order to reintegrate them into your personality.

Progress now

Make a list of the attributes that most infuriate you in others. Your list will tell you a lot about the shadow side of your personality.

THE GOLDEN SHADOW

The shadow is often thought of as negative, but in fact it provides an unrivalled opportunity to improve not only your coaching skills but also your personal development in general. Another aspect of your shadow is the 'golden' shadow – positive traits which, given the opportunity for greater expression, provide the greatest potential for growth. You can most easily become aware of your golden shadow by thinking of people you admire, and reflecting on what it is about them that draws you to them – perhaps their natural warmth, their generosity, or their clarity of purpose. Whatever it is, you will find that strengthening and utilizing that part of your personality will make you both a more skilled coach and a more rounded person.

DEVELOPING AS A COACH

One of the best ways of taking your coaching to the next level is to make a tape recording of some of your sessions and play them back to review your own performance. If you decide to do this, be sure to obtain the permission of your client and to explain the purpose of your request.

Getting someone to supervise your coaching is a very practical way of developing your skills as a coach as it gives you an entirely new perspective and to learn from the experience of being coached by someone who has a different style or approach to you. If you are working in-company, you can ask another internal coach to take on this role. If you are an external coach you can use your network of contacts to find the right person for you.

There are many books on the subject of coaching and personal development that will expand your thinking. There are also coaching courses which not only give you the chance to get in touch with current thinking about the subject but also allow you to meet and share ideas with other coaches.

WHY EVERY COACH NEEDS A COACH

Having a coach yourself has a multiplicity of advantages. First and foremost it gives you more clarity and reality about your 'stuff' which means this is less likely to impact on your clients. You also learn from the experience of being coached by someone who has a different style or approach to you.

You might also consider who else could be involved with your development. Some people work in partnership with a group of coaches. This can be a bonus in a number of ways. There will be times when you may not be the right coach for someone. If you work within a team or at least know other coaches you can recommend should you find yourself in this situation it can be very useful.

TRANSFERRING YOUR SKILLS

Coaching skills are a valuable asset which can be used to transform relationships in every area of your life. Some of the skills can be used in numerous ways as part of your working life, such as chairing a meeting where it is essential you listen well and draw people's views out through the use of questions. Wherever you come across conflict, coaching skills can help to soothe the situation, especially if you are a third party who has been called in to mediate. In any situation taking a coaching approach is going to mean you build rapport with people and take time to get a feel for what they have to say about things.

COACHING YOUR FAMILY AND FRIENDS

Once coaching is part of your life you may find you start to coach whenever someone presents you with an issue. It's easy for coaching to become so much part of you that you can't stop. Be aware that sometimes your friends or family members just want you to listen or even offer a solution. It is important to know when to coach and when not to.

If you are a man living with a woman, your coaching skills can be very useful in enhancing your relationship. Men are often given to trying to solve problems, when all women want is to feel heard and understood. They like to talk about their experiences and the emotions attached to them and don't want or need anyone else to fix the problem for them. John Gray's *Men are from Mars, Women are from Venus* clearly highlights this difference between the sexes.

Women coaches, on the other hand, may find the ability to be comfortable with silence, among other things, welcome when their partner becomes uncommunicative. Rather than persist in questioning, you can wait patiently until it's the right time for your partner to engage with you again.

CHILD'S PLAY

Telling your children what to do comes naturally to most parents – but it's not always effective. While all children need clear boundaries, using your coaching skills to encourage them to make the most of their own resources to sort out problems, rather than always running to you for answers, will help them develop self-reliance and with it self-confidence. And while it cannot be claimed that a coaching approach will solve all your problems through the tortuous teenage years, it may be the best way to at least keep channels of communication open and maintain a positive relationship for the future.

SHARE YOUR COACHING SKILLS

One of the best ways to hone your skills as a coach is to help other people to develop theirs. Once you have developed your abilities, you can start passing them on. This can be by setting up 'sharing' sessions, where you can talk about your experiences of coaching. If you work in-company you may find it easier to buddy up with one or two other coaches and swap notes and ideas on an informal basis from time to time. If you are perhaps one of a few people experimenting with coaching in your company, you may be able to create a forum to talk about it and play a part in establishing a more thorough and integrated coaching culture.

CHAPTER 12

Your Next Step

There is a vitality, a life force, an energy, a quickening that is translated through you into action, and because there is only one of you in all time, this expression is unique. And if you block it, it will never exist through any other medium and will be lost.

MARTHA GRAHAM

None of us knows what the next change is going to be, what unexpected opportunity is just around the corner, waiting a few months or a few years to change all the tenor of our lives.

KATHLEEN NORRIS

PULLING IT ALL TOGETHER

In Chapter 7 we discussed the importance of making the final session with a client a 'completion' session, of looking back together over the course of the coaching relationship as a means of helping the client integrate their learning at the conscious level. This book has been coaching you to improve your knowledge, skills and understanding. This final session gives you the opportunity of 'completing' – of looking back in order to see how far you have come and what you have achieved.

WHERE DO YOU GO FROM HERE?

Having taken stock, the time is now right to plan the next leg of your journey. If you are coaching in-company you may be wondering how you can help develop the skills of other managers in your company or be curious about the best way to create a coaching culture. You may be thinking about setting up in business as an independent coach or expanding your existing coaching practice by either employing other coaches or attracting associates to work for you. Or you might simply want to turn your attention to another skill area all together, such as leadership.

Progress now

Allow yourself at least half an hour to reflect on the following questions. You don't have to answer them all, and you don't need to go through them in any particular order. It's not a definitive list. They are intended merely as prompts to get you thinking about what have been the high points and key learnings for you.

- What's important to me about coaching?
- What are my natural strengths as a coach?
- Where do I sometimes hold myself back?
- What are the key things I've learnt about the coaching process?
- What am I most proud of?
- Which three changes could I make that would improve my coaching?

Progress now

Spend a few minutes thinking about where you are now. Next spend some time considering where you want to be. Use all your senses to build a complete picture.

Once you have done this stop and think. What would be half way to achieving it? If it still seems far away, break it down further by working out what a quarter of the way there would be like.

What is the first step you can take to move you forward to reach the mid point? What beliefs would it be useful for you to have? What support is there available to you? Who might you be able to call upon for help? What might stop you? What steps can you take to minimize the risk of this happening?

Once you have made your way to the mid point you can apply the same process to moving on to the next stage. Alternatively you can use any of the techniques, strategies and ideas in this book.

CREATIVE INTEGRATION

You might also like to create a picture, metaphor or story which represents the main points you have learned from reading this book and completing the activities. As an added incentive on this the authors will offer ten free places a year on their Infinite Potential Coaching Course for stories, pictures or metaphors that they consider to be truly creative. Send a copy of your activity to us at competition@infinitepotential.co.uk. You can also contact the authors for details of future courses, both open and bespoke, executive and life coaching, coaching supervision and further advice on how to introduce a coaching culture into your company. Please go to our website http://www.infinitepotential.co.uk or email us at coaching@infinitepotential.co.uk

References

Blanchard, Ken and Sheldon Bowles (1998) *Gung Ho!* HarperCollins Business.

Dilts, Robert (2002) *Alpha Leadership*. John Wiley.

Flaherty, James (1999) *Coaching: Evoking Excellence in Others.* Butterworth Heinemann.

Gallwey, Tim (2000) *The Inner Game of Work*. Orion Business Books.

Gray, John. *Men are from Mars, Women are from Venus.* Vermillion.

Industrial Society (September 1999) *Managing Best Practice: Coaching*. Report No. 63. The Industrial Society, London.

Robbins, Anthony (1992) *Awaken the Giant Within.* Simon & Schuster.

Sher, Barbara (1979) *Wishcraft: How to Get What You Really Want*. Ballantine.

Whitmore, John (1992; 2nd edn 1996) *Coaching for Performance*. Nicholas Brearley Publishing.

Whitworth, Laura, Henry Kimsey-House and Phil Sandahl (1998) *Co-active Coaching*. Davies-Black Publishing.

Williamson, Marianne (1992) *A Return to Love*. HarperCollins.

NOTES

NOTES

NOTES

NOTES

NOTES

NOTES